WHERE THE SHORELINE USED TO BE

PUFFIN BOOKS

UK | USA | Canada | Ireland | Australia
India | New Zealand | South Africa | China

Penguin Books is part of the Penguin Random House group of companies whose addresses can be found at global.penguinrandomhouse.com.

First published by Penguin Australia Pty Ltd, 2016

10 9 8 7 6 5 4 3 2 1

Cover and text design by Bruno Herfst © Penguin Australia Pty Ltd, 2016
Typeset in Trump Mediaeval by Bruno Herfst
Colour separation by Splitting Image Colour Studio, Clayton, Victoria
Printed and bound in Australia by Griffin Press, an accredited ISO AS/NZS 14001 Environmental Management Systems printer.

National Library of Australia Cataloguing-in-Publication data available.

ISBN: 978 0 14 357322 7

puffin.com.au

WHERE THE SHORELINE USED TO BE

AN ANTHOLOGY FROM AUSTRALIA AND BEYOND

EDITED BY
SUSAN LA MARCA
& PAM MACINTYRE

PUFFIN BOOKS

CONTENTS

INTRODUCTION

Where the Shoreline Used to Be is a loose companion to our first anthology *Things a Map Won't Show You*. Both are collections of imaginative works in a range of short forms. Short stories, poems and song lyrics, despite or because of their brevity, can stretch and challenge readers. While the first anthology is aimed at early secondary students, this new collection embraces an older audience, showcasing gritty writing and the range of experiences typical for the later years of secondary school.

'A story gives us heroes and heroines to copy. A story sets examples. A story cautions. A story points us to the stars. A story tells us that we are not alone. Stories make us honourable members of the human family and tell us that dreams can come true.'

PAUL JENNINGS, author, *Knowing Readers*

Narrative shapes experiences for readers. It helps us to make sense of our own lives and gives patterns to our experiences.

An anthology allows for variety and enables us to offer choice. As readers dip in and out, we hope they will find stories that engage them, but others that trouble or challenge them. And something that encourages them to see the world differently or to consider other ways of experiencing it. Each poem, story and song could be explored individually, and there are opportunities to compare one with another in terms of content and/or form.

For many years we have both worked in various roles, hoping to connect stories and readers: talking and writing about story, analysing and thinking about narrative and ultimately enjoying and immersing ourselves in wonderful stories. It is a pleasure to be able to think about what pieces, and which writers, we would like to share, what forms and styles we would like to put in the hands of readers. We are pleased to introduce the work of new writers whose works are published here for the first time, as well as original work from established writers whose shorter fiction is equally as potent as their longer works. Favourite stories and recollections from existing collections have also been chosen for further sharing.

Diversity of genre, style and form is central to this anthology. Providing variety and exposing readers to different narrative forms celebrates the power of story and puts formidable writing in the hands of readers. We hope that our aim of offering readers pleasure and enjoyment in their reading will support such experiences in the classroom and beyond, and allow readers to experience the joys of reading.

'Reading is a provocative act;
it makes things happen.'
AIDAN CHAMBERS, author

SHAUN TAN

Shaun is an artist, writer and filmmaker based in Melbourne. His illustrated books for both adults and children include *The Rabbits, The Red Tree, Rules of Summer, Tales from Outer Suburbia* and the acclaimed wordless novel *The Arrival.* In 2011 he received the Astrid Lindgren Memorial Award in Sweden and an Academy Award for his short animated film *The Lost Thing*.

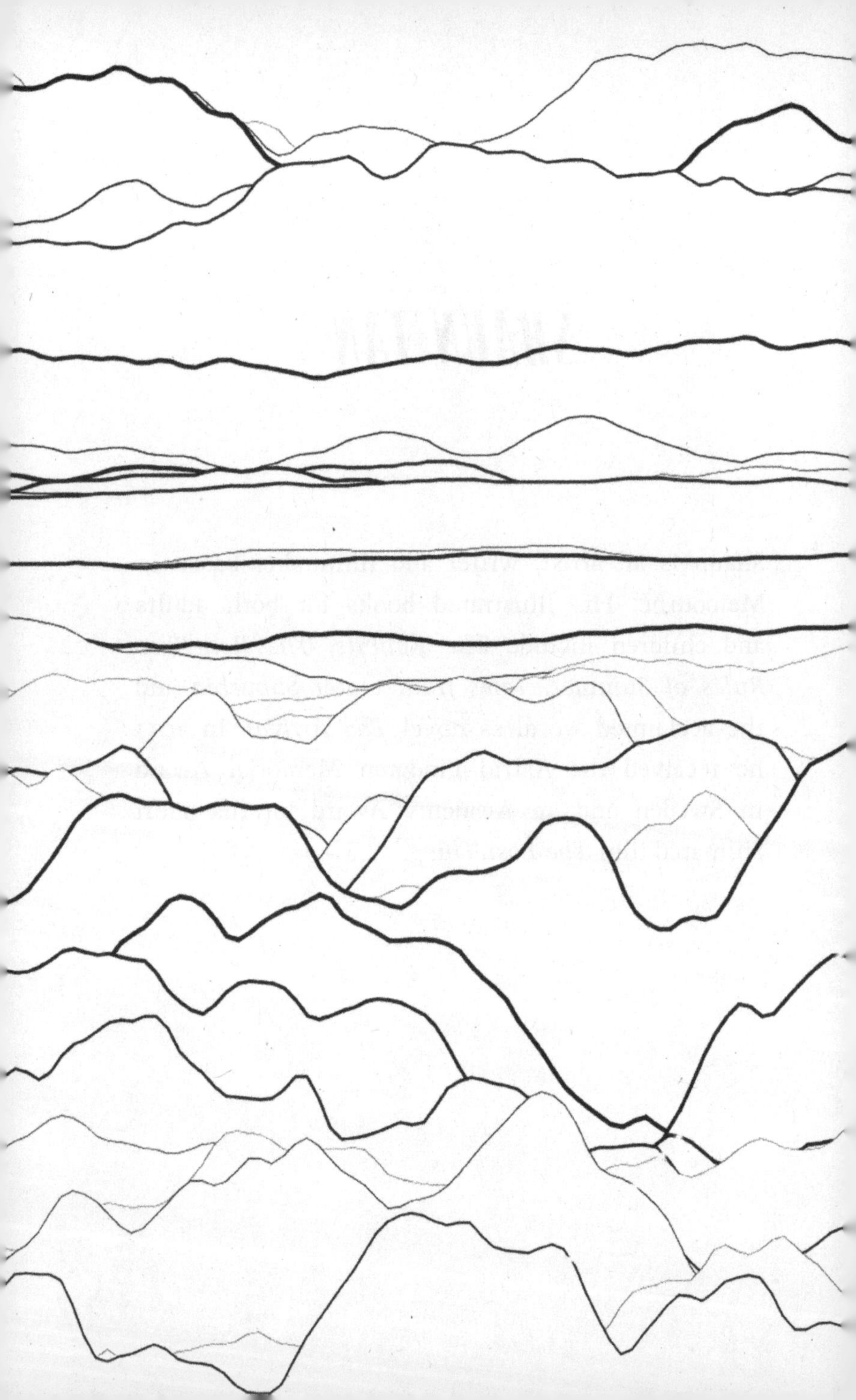

THE BUTTERFLIES

The butterflies came at lunchtime. Not millions, billions or even trillions but a number beyond counting, beyond even the concept of counting, so people on the street were relieved of any estimation. By people on the street, I mean everyone. Literally *everyone*. No earthquake, fire or terrorist attack could flush so many out of cars, apartments, subways, restaurants, hotels, stores, banks, museums, hospitals, schools, parliaments and offices. None had ever experienced such inexplicable, joyful urgency.

And as if in response, the butterflies came to us, descending from dizzying heights like spring blossoms of every imaginable colour and pattern. Gliding, skipping, fluttering around our ears in soundless wonder.

We were standing so still, shoulder-to-shoulder, stalled as traffic on bridges, every breath held and every eye open, waiting for the weightless blessing of tiny insects. *Look! Look! There on your shoulder, your arm, your knee, your head! Hold still! Don't move! Look at this one right here on my nose!* And for that briefest of moments, faces and palms to the sky, we did not ask why. The chatter in our heads fell silent, the endless ticker tape of voice-over narrative, always prying things apart for cause and effect, sign and symbol, some kind of useful meaning or value or portent – it all just stopped, and the butterflies came to us.

Later they would leave, technicolour clouds billowing up and drifting away to the west. Later our minds would quickly snap back to factory settings and the chatter would resume. *Was this an omen of something good or bad? A plague? A system out of whack? A divine message? A lesson in chaos? What does it mean? What does it mean?* Later we would study photo and video evidence with furrowed brows, listen to media analysis, consult scripture and meteorology, look at maps, graphs, stats and bell curves. Later we would worry.

But for now, for that briefest of all moments, we did not ask why. We thought of nothing but the butterflies, the butterflies settling on our heads, on the heads of friends and family, on everyone we knew and everyone we didn't, on the whole city all at once. *Don't move,* we whispered, wishing it could last forever. *Hold still! Hold still! Hold still!*

TRUDY WHITE

Trudy likes to draw and paint pictures and write stories and poetry. She lives in a country town in Victoria with a little girl and a big dog. They have more books than chairs in their house, and they spend a lot of time reading. Especially the dog.

PENCIL

Who, Brenda? She collects all kinds of pencils. Has done since she was three, apparently. She went to the Happy Hamburger Hut where they gave her a puzzle placemat and a grey lead pencil to draw with. Red outside with the H.H.H motif on. As big as your little finger.

Oh yes, she could have gone the other way! Sometimes she talks about the beginnings of her collection, how things might have been if she'd taken the placemat home.

Now, when you go to Brenda's house, you'll see how neatly she stores them, all set out in that new extension. She's updating the data on them now with a grant from the government.

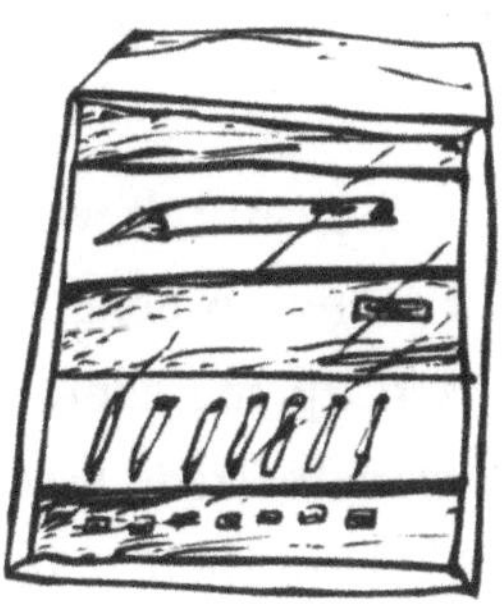

You can read the notes pasted

on the glass cases, but I can tell you some bits you won't read. There's her first box of coloured pencils on show, in a tin, with gold numbers on them. Well, she wouldn't let anyone else in Grade Four use them. At lunchtime, she would go back to the classroom, sneak open the tin and check they were still in order. We all dreamed of what we'd like to do with them.

She only drew sparingly, sensible pictures worthy of using up pencil for. Odd, the way they've all been used up the same length. I don't know how she got through Grade Five, myself.

Then there's the pencil stub retrieved from her

baby sister's esophagus. You can imagine Brenda throwing a fit so the surgeon would let her keep it, can't you?

Make sure you get a good look at the pencil used by Captain Cook to draw the first map of Australia. She bought it at a Christies' auction only recently. What do you mean, how do they know?

Brenda's diversified her collection since she moved back here. She's got more than your classic old wood and grey-lead – I mean, graphite. (She would hate to hear me say that after this long.)

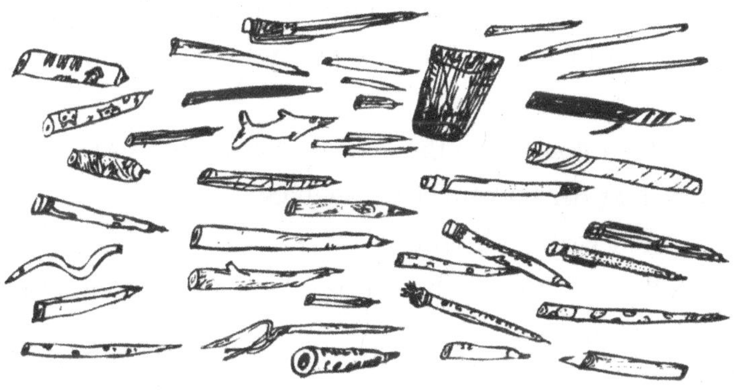

Remember the clear plastic pencils that you loaded with little leads like bullets? They were big in the seventies. We all had them until they were banned because of people like Brenda's sister. Brenda kept a whole range. Hidden in a Dunlop runners box.

She's got your novelty pencils – multi-coloured in the one stick (that's industry talk for pencil) – thick sticks, round sticks, a stick made from a branch, tiny coloured sticks, small as matches in a fairy pouch. Pencils from every country you could name.

They have led her into trouble, though. It takes a rare person to understand such a passion.

Her first boyfriend was a carpenter. She used to go on to me about his flat square pencil and chalk bag. I never thought it would last. I was happy for her when she met an architect who introduced her to silver mechanical pencils with built-in rubbers. But he diverted into computers and Brenda refused to update to mouses. That's why she's stayed single for so long.

When you get to the last cabinet at Brenda's, have a look at the bottom three shelves.

No, I won't tell you!

Oh, all right: her new husband's sharpener collection.

AMIE KAUFMAN

Amie is a *New York Times* bestselling author of young adult fiction. Her work has been published in 17 countries and is in development for film and TV. Her first series, co-authored with Meagan Spooner, began with *These Broken Stars*, which won the Aurealis Award for Best YA Novel in 2013 and was named Huffington Post's best YA novel of the year in 2013. Her new series, co-authored with Jay Kristoff, began with *Illuminae*.

Raised in Australia and Ireland, Amie lives in Melbourne with her husband and rescue dog. She's been telling family stories as long as she can remember, and she never plans on stopping.

I SWEAR THIS PART IS TRUE

What you are about to read is a true story.

It is also a family story, which means it isn't true at all.

If you know anything about family stories, you know the more times they're told, the fuzzier they become around the edges. Embellishments are added to suit the audience, jokes creep in because the storyteller thinks this part needs a little something extra, or angles change because someone doesn't look so good in that version of events. We choose the day or occasion on which we'll share a particular tale, make it quick or draw it out, carefully select our audience. Every family does this.

We define ourselves by our stories – with our words

and our choices we can create our own identity, show everyone around us who we are.

We are our own personal myth makers, every one of us. This is why, when it comes to our stories, the manner of the telling matters very much. Tell it right, and you can shape and create a small part of yourself.

So this is a true story, and it's a family story, and this is the way I tell it.

My father had a series of unusual pets when he was a kid. He had a very large tortoise, which made the world's slowest (yet inexplicably successful) jailbreak. He had a carpet snake that vanished for six months, only to be found hibernating on the top shelf in the tool shed.

And then there was the kangaroo. This story is about the kangaroo.

My father was one of four brothers, all of them tall, lanky, handsome teenagers who got up to more mischief than their parents ever dreamt. They raced in borrowed cars, crept out for late-night adventures and forged letters to their headmaster. My dad learnt to ride a motorbike in the backyard on the end of a lunging rope, round in circles like a young horse. He was the youngest, which meant – as it often does – that he was the subject of more than one experiment by his older brothers. It also meant he remembered things differently to my uncles. Sometimes he was right, and remembered more clearly. Sometimes he was wrong – he hadn't been told the whole story, or worse, he had been sent to bed before the fun started, though there are plenty of tales that feature him clad in his pyjamas, rescued from that fate.

By the time this story came around, all four boys were in their teens. Everyone still has a different version of how the kangaroo came to join the family, but on one thing they all agree these days – my uncle Darrell brought it home. (I think we'll make it *her* for this telling – see how the personal touches creep in?) She was orphaned and alone, and depending on who's telling the story, her mother was shot, or hit by a car, though everyone agrees Darrell fished her out of her mum's pouch, and the four boys gave her a second chance at life one summer holidays.

She was a tiny, skinny thing, stretching from about Dad's shoulder to his elbow, with feet almost as long as the whole rest of her body. She needed feeding and warming, raising and teaching, and though the four of them could take a car around a hairpin turn, win a game of pool and dock a boat in the dark, between them they didn't know how to make so much as a bowl of porridge.

These days, they'd have been one quick internet search away from 'how to raise a kangaroo' or 'wildlife sanctuary', but this was a long time ago, and they knew it was either them, or nothing.

They also knew immediately they had to hide her, because there was no way my grandparents were going to approve of a kangaroo in the house. Luckily for Joey, as she was quickly (if not creatively) named, her four new caretakers had a long and storied history of concealing things from their parents.

The first challenges were working out where she'd sleep and what she'd eat. For her bed, they found a backpack that they lined with woollen scarves from their school uniforms, which wouldn't be needed for another couple of terms. They hung it on a doorknob, and within hours Joey had learnt to clamber into it. She'd give a small hop and throw herself forward, landing head first with her big feet sticking out. The feet would give a wriggle and a kick, then disappear inside the backpack. A moment later, her head would pop out the opening, check all was well, then withdraw once more.

The food was trickier – nobody knew what a kangaroo ate. In the end, they settled for a mix of milk (which came with cream floating on top in those days, fat being essential to babies) and grass (which it was my dad's job to harvest from the back garden every day when nobody was looking.) Joey settled in happily with her four new caretakers, quick to snuggle her small, furry body into laps, nuzzling the crooks of their arms, and nibbling the grass they offered her.

After a few days, they thought she might like to go outside. They waited until their parents had left for lunch with friends and the housekeeper had departed to do the weekly shopping, then carried the backpack into the garden, where Joey could poke out her head and enjoy some sunshine. It took only a few moments before the little brown ears appeared, twitching curiously, followed by her nose. My uncle Ian laid the backpack on the grass carefully, and Joey eased free of it, with that front-to-back hop that kangaroos use when they're moving slowly. Weight forward onto the front paws, slowly, slowly, then a lolloping hop with the back legs. She did it again – slowly, slowly, hop – and then again.

And then she took off across the garden with quick,

confident bounds, seeming unaffected by gravity as she soared through the air. The boys laughed like proud parents – *look at her go!* – then laughter turned to shouts as Joey found the path up the side of the house and raced toward the front garden.

Four bodies crowded up the side path in pursuit, ricocheting off the house, the fence and each other, bursting into the front garden just in time to see Joey disappear through the gate. They tore down the street together, legs pumping and lungs burning, and on one thing, every person who tells this story agrees: the only reason they caught that kangaroo was because she decided she was done with the game.

My dad was sent to fetch the backpack. Panting and sobered, they carried her home. For the first time, the shadow of the future fell square upon them. What would they do when she grew up? She wouldn't put up with a backpack in a bedroom forever. How would they find enough room for her, and how would they continue to hide her?

The last of these questions was to be answered much sooner than they'd imagined.

But first, a word about my grandmother. I never met Grandmother Lilian, but I am named for her (my middle name), and all my life I've sought out stories about her. The stories tend in the same direction; they say she was quick-witted, well-educated, always immaculately put together, and that my grandfather was utterly devoted to her – and she to him.

There was nothing about her, however, that prepared her four sons for the day they came home to find her immaculately clad self wearing a neat and rather stylish apron, with a large pocket sewn onto the front and a baby kangaroo tucked into that pocket. *Were they caught, or had they just caught out their mother? Just how much trouble were they in?*

'Oh dear,' she said, surveying their stunned faces. 'You thought I didn't know. Mrs Cohen saw you chasing it down the street last Thursday, so I thought I'd better brave your bedrooms and see if it was true.'

As she spoke, Joey stuck her head out of the pocket, and my grandmother absently scratched her between the ears. Their furry little charge had won another heart.

The boys imagined that with their secret out in the open, life might become a little easier, but they were only partly correct. My grandmother did help them hide Joey from my grandfather, and occasionally consented to babysitting duties, but she made quite clear that the boys had parental responsibilities now. They had brought Joey into their lives, so were the ones who had to make it work.

As the summer wore on, the trading of chores and negotiating for babysitting began to wear on the boys.

There were fewer chances to race in cars and sail on the bay. Over the summer holidays, all four boys also had romance on their minds, and having to get home from dates in time to feed the kangaroo was wearing thin.

To make matters worse, Joey was still growing. She daily became more confident, wriggling out of the backpack and hopping around whichever bedroom she was in, careening off the bed, the dressing table, and eyeballing the green grass of freedom through the window. The question of what they'd do when the summer holidays ended loomed larger.

But for every little mishap – like the time Joey tried to eat a lemon cake and threw up on the kitchen floor, she offered enough excitement to push the problems of the future out of their minds. Sure, she accidentally released the handbrake on the car, sending it rolling slowly but unstoppably back into the street, and sure, my uncle Ian thought he was going to have a heart attack as he ran out of the house and after the car, throwing himself through the open passenger window to yank on the brake again, stopping it inches from the Cohens' Rolls Royce . . . but she was a lot of fun.

One time the boys clipped a piece off the chain-link tennis court fence to use as a barrier at the top of the stairs, so Joey could hop up and down the hallway safely. She joyously cleared it in one bound, heading downstairs and straight for the china cabinet. 'Stop her,' Darrell yelled, jumping the fence to chase after her. The bad news for Darrell was that Ian and my dad did the same thing so the three of them fell down the stairs in a tangle of arms and legs.

Graeme was the most scientific of the four, so he had a faster idea – he knocked down the fence and rode it all the way to the bottom on his hands and knees, using his brothers for a soft landing, then jumping over them to grab the kangaroo.

'Anything broken?' Darrell asked, from the bottom of the pile.

There was a pause as everyone checked their arms and legs.

'Don't think so.'

'Philip's on my head; get off.'

Kangaroo under one arm, Graeme slowly pulled them apart, and the four of them climbed to their feet, looking at one another.

'I think you just invented staircase skiing,' my dad said to Graeme. 'Can I go next?'

Joey's adventures didn't stop there. One time my grandmother, wearing a cardigan buttoned over her Joey apron, answered the front door to a travelling salesman. As the man talked, a small, brown head slowly wormed through the gap between two buttons to stare unblinkingly at him. 'And have you considered . . . I . . . ah . . .' He trailed off, staring at the alien growing out of my grandmother's chest, his eyes bulging.

'Yes?' she said, politely attentive, as if nothing was happening. She wasn't that fond of door-to-door salesmen.

'I'd best be going,' he said, taking two steps backward, then turning to run.

'Don't forget to close the gate!' she called after him, waving.

And finally, there was the day my grandfather caught the boys as he made his way out the door for a game of cards. 'I think you should fix that hole in the tennis court fence,' he said casually, the words sending ice straight down their spines. He must have known they'd cut it, or he'd have asked the gardener to fix it. *But did he know why?*

'Sure, Dad,' my uncle Graeme stuttered, on behalf of all of them.

'Good,' he said, turning away. 'That kangaroo upstairs really needs to stretch its legs and the tennis court will be just the place.'

They stood speechless as he strolled off.

They fixed the tennis court fence, and Joey took to exercising on the asphalt and grass in great, long leaps, but they weren't sure it was enough. She'd bounce over to them and ask to play, staying just out of reach when they chased her, tempting them into games of tag, which left them breathless and her as fresh as when they started.

She'd clamber into laps when she didn't fit in the backpack any more, snuggling into their arms, her heart thumping steadily beneath her soft fur. Soon she could be trusted to hop around the back garden without taking off down the street, and she'd lounge in the sun, scratching her ribs with one paw, eyes half-closed in bliss.

But sometimes the kangaroo would bury her face against the boys when the noise around her got too loud, or – startled by the backfiring of a car nearby – thump her back foot on the ground to warn them of danger. She found it more difficult to get down the stairs now, so she rarely climbed them, but now and again she'd bound up, checking behind doors for her too-small backpack, her safe place.

The truth was, she needed her own mob of kangaroos – and a mob of boys couldn't substitute forever. She needed more than the Kaufman boys could give her. They had created their own story about Joey, and told it to each other all summer – the kangaroo who thought she was a human, the kangaroo who loved the garden, loved to play tag, loved to ride in the car and stick her head out the window.

And perhaps those stories were all true, but there was another story forcing its way to the surface, whether they wanted it or not.

The kangaroo who was all alone.

They all knew it, and eventually the first of them said it aloud. Joey needed more than they could give her, and if they loved her, it was time to prove it.

In the end, my grandfather made a phone call, and they crammed into the car together. My grandparents took the front seat, and the four boys squeezed into the back with Joey, dodging her tail as she poked her head out the window to enjoy the breeze. They drove across town to Parkville, and around to the back gate, where a zookeeper was waiting to meet them. 'You're the third this month,' he said, winning Joey's love almost instantly with a handful of chaff. 'It's the season for it.'

She did look after them as they drove away, but not for as long as they had feared – or perhaps hoped. Then the car turned the corner, and she was gone from sight.

And that's the story of the time my dad had a kangaroo for the summer. If you visit Melbourne Zoo, it's possible you might just meet Joey's descendants lazing about in the sun. Or maybe not.

That's the thing about family stories. I couldn't say for sure.

SCOT GARDNER

Scot has been writing for young people for most of his life. He lives with his wife in country Victoria – their three kids have grown up and left home. He is fascinated by solar panels, wild country and the life cycle of gordiids. If he wasn't a writer, he'd build underground houses.

ANOTHER THEORY OF RELATIVITY

Ryan Griffiths
Year 10 Philosophy, Mr Denver

Major report
The Relative Nature of Life

I'm sixteen and I know that the experience of life is mostly a relative concept. Nothing is truly good or bad, hot or cold, wet or dry, happy or sad. These are all ideas compared and contrasted with other ideas. I know it sounds a bit ~~philos~~ ~~intelle~~ fancy, but stick with me – it'll be worth it.

So if an old fart drops into the train seat next to you, smelling of earwax and says, 'Jeeze, it's cold out there,' you can say, 'Cold compared to what?' Cold compared to the morning you barefooted it to the car through the snow? Ice-age cold? Even the fact that he's an old fart is a relative term – old compared to what? Old compared to you, maybe, but not old compared to the pyramids, which aren't particularly old compared to some of the rock art in the Kimberley, which in turn are spring chickens compared to the dinosaur I just made up – *Dinosaurus oldfarticus*. She just had her 150 millionth birthday. Happy birthday to you. Hip hooray.

My step-dad bought me a speedo for my mountain bike last birthday and I tested it out on Veno's hill. I mean, that hill is *steep* (compared to the ocean you can see from the top of it, anyway). Belting down the slope, it feels like I'm going a little over 300 kilometres per hour. If my speedo's correct, it's actually 72.2 kph. I've slept in the back of my stepfather's car going faster than that – 110. On the dot. When I flew to Malawi to spend a summer doing aid work with my biological dad, the in-flight stats said we were travelling at 890 kilometres per hour. I slept at that speed too, but not as well as the dude in the seat next to me who snored like a pig farm.

It's all relative.

No, Amanda, you are not 'fat' and your boobs are not 'too big' – you are what you are.

Don't get me started on boobs.

And whatever you do, don't shake your head behind Megan – the Year 8 chick in the wheelchair – and say, 'Poor girl.' I know for a fact she hates that shit. She didn't pick up cerebral palsy on sale at Target, but she understands relativity and sometimes sees CP as a gift. She reckons she knows able-bodied people who suffer more than she does. Megan, of all people, has a special slant on the individual and fickle nature of happiness and, for the most part, she chooses happy. For a Year 8, she's pretty smart.

How can you 'hate' maths? Compared to what? English? Being beaten on the bum with a car aerial? I've tried all three and I think maths has its plusses and minuses.

;-)

I wonder how much happier we would be if we got into the habit of reminding ourselves that happiness is relative? I know if I reminded you, it would take about three minutes before you felt like stabbing me in the arm with your HB pencil.

Still, pain is relative too. You could have gone for the eye or smacked my sensitive gentleman potatoes. The fact that pain is relative isn't much consolation when you're hurting. That's probably the same with true poverty too. Let's imagine a dude. We'll call him Billy. No relation to Billy the skater dude in Year 9,

I swear. Have you seen his shoes? They're all sock underneath and he won't have money for a new pair until next semester – that's six weeks of winter to kick through. During the drought in Malawi, people boiled and ate the skins of animals that would have normally been used to make shoes. There was so little food and the land had been stripped so bare that people were fighting over goat skins. 'Billy' might know the cold better than most, but he won't have to eat his shoes. We'll make sure of that.

And finally, I arrive at the soft underparts of this idea of life being relative.

We're all relatives. (See what I did there? Poet.)

Our ancestors – I mean, absolutely every single one – strolled out of Africa a few years before my grandmother got her licence, but we kind of conveniently forget that from time to time. Who would lock their relatives and their kids in a detention centre? What sort of monster straps explosives to himself and blows up 50 relatives on a train? A relatively misguided one, IMHO.

And if you remember back to the start of this relatively long-winded rant (to the bit about the old fart) you'll see that I cunningly inferred that time is, in fact, relative. That means if you think about time only in human terms, then you miss out on the bigger story of life.

Think like a rock for a minute.

Think like a chunk of basalt born from the guts of the planet when the seas were made entirely of lava. Man, you've seen a *lot*. You were cool before it became trendy on the surface of the Earth. You were there when hydrogen and oxygen got married on *Neighbours*. You let their baby (that's water) lick your face, then, wham, bam, thank you Ma'am, water's got unicellular kids of her own and they're hanging out together playing their photosynthesisers. Next thing you know, those innocent little plants have become total *animals*. They think they're so clever with their oxygen breathing and their sexual reproduction and their opposable thumbs, but we know different, don't we, Rock? Rock?? Hellooooo? She's gone all shy now the spotlight's on her, but do you see her point?

From a rock's perspective we're ALL related.

All the minerals, plants and animals.

And if we're related to the trees and rocks and air and water and animals, how can we justify destroying all our relatives' one and only home? Um, reality check – it's our one and only home too.

Rock has seen every step along the way to the infinitely complex expressions of life we now know, like Billy's shoe, Megan's wheelchair and Amanda's perfectly adequate boobs. Rock didn't have to make up some imaginary friend with superpowers to *create* all this stuff; she was there. She saw it all evolving.

That's not relative; that's *absolute*.

We are all one.

Do you get that? I feel like writing it one more time for effect, but I won't because that would be labouring the point.

Just one planet, and we all sprung from it. Take it back another step and you'll see that our pointy rock's ancestors were the stuff that all the stars are made of. And we're probably a relatively complex arrangement of starstuff, capable of quite complex thoughts like, 'Chicken or beef?', '*South Park* or *Simpsons*?' and 'Amanda's boobs'. I think if you watched the insides of your eyelids for about the same amount of time it takes for your burger to be made, just contemplating the interconnectedness of all living and non-living parts of the planet and our origins as starstuff, the things that make life 'bad' or 'good' become clearer.

For example, some people have holes in their shoes and others have multiple pairs so there are *pockets* of relative wealth and poverty. If I offer Billy my hand-painted Dunlop Volleys, I get to feel kindness and 'Billy' gets to feel dry socks and our oneness is affirmed like a practical and cosmic high-five. There are pockets of relative hunger and pockets of obesity, pockets of ignorance and pockets of relative wisdom, sometimes in the one classroom. We've come a long way since we were rocks. Well, some of us have.

How do I know all this shit?

Well, I'm relatively gay. That might come as a shock for some – you can close your mouth now, Benson – but for others, like most of the class and my stepdad, who, it turns out, personifies 'pocket of relative wisdom', my coming out was a simple statement of fact. My hair is brown. My eyes are blue. I quite like boys.

I say 'relatively gay' because human sexual preference could be the poster child for relative thinking. I can still appreciate perfectly adequate boobs (*cough*, *Amanda*), but go gaga for certain butts dancing in denim. There's a whole rainbow of experience between gay and straight and you're not nailed to the rainbow, you can move about a bit if you want to find out how you're wired. Even gender isn't absolute – we're not just boys and girls and you're free to sit where you like there too.

It turns out my biological father, while a big-hearted and generous man, believes gender, sexual preference and identity are absolutes. Turns out he's also quite handy with a car aerial. A couple of thousand years ago his imaginary friend dictated a book to a few desert-dwelling relatives who were still excited about the invention of the wheelbarrow and my father treats it like . . . well . . . gospel. He's not alone. There are lots of people who believe their imaginary friend is the *best* and anybody who thinks differently is sick in the head and should be killed. That's a big pocket of relative ignorance, and part of me wants to just let them be. But if we're all truly related and born of the same starstuff, then it feels like there's a growth on the back of my hand when they blah blah their bullshit. I want to get it checked out. Perhaps it will wash off, but it might be something serious.

I don't know about you, but I want to live as large as I can for as long as I can in this wonderland. If you're brain-dead, there's no coming back from that – that's an absolute – but until you die you have an infinite variety of ways to muck around with all the knobs and buttons on the mixing deck of life. You can continue the tradition of filling pockets of ignorance with your relative wisdom. You can sow happy-thought seeds wherever you go and help others remember that we're things of great beauty, rocketing through the cosmos on a thing of great beauty.

KATE MILLER-HEIDKE

Kate Miller-Heidke is an award-winning and critically acclaimed singer-songwriter who grew up in Queensland. She trained as a classical singer but chose to focus on alternative pop music. *Caught in the Crowd,* co-written with her husband, guitarist and fellow singer-songwriter Keir Nuttall, won the Grand Prize in the 2008 International Songwriting Competition. They were the first Australians ever to win the grand prize.

The song is based on Kate's own experiences of bullying at school.

CAUGHT IN THE CROWD

There was a guy at my school when
I was in high school
We'd ride side by side in the morning on our bicycles
Never even spoken or faced each other
But on the last hill we'd race each other

When we reached the racks, we'd
each go our own way
I wasn't in his classes, I didn't know his name
When we finally got to speak, he
just stared at his feet
And mumbled a sentence that ended with James

I was young and caught in the crowd
I didn't know then what I know now
I was dumb and I was proud and I'm sorry

If I could go back, do it again
I'd be someone you could call friend
Please, please believe that I'm sorry

Well, he was quite a big guy, kinda shy and quiet
When the kids called him weird, he
  didn't try to deny it
Every lunchtime he'd spend walking by himself
'Round the boundary of the grounds
  'til he heard the bell

Well, one day I found him, joined him on his walk
We were silent for a while until we started to talk
I told him my family were fighting in court
He said his step-dad and him always fought

We talked about music, he was into punk
Told me all the bands that I liked were junk
I said I'd never heard the songs the Sex Pistols sang
I laughed back at him and then the bell rang

I was young and caught in the crowd
I didn't know then what I know now
I was dumb and I was proud and I'm sorry

If I could go back, do it again
I'd be someone you could call friend
Please, please believe that I'm sorry

It was after school in the afternoon
The corridors were crowded as we
  came out of the rooms
Three guys I knew pushed him into the cement
Threw away his bag and said he had no friends

He yelled that he did and he looked around
Tried getting up but they pushed him on down
That's when he saw me, called out my name
And I turned my back and just walked away
Yeah, I turned my back and just walked away

I was young and caught in the crowd
I didn't know then what I know now
I was dumb and I was proud and I'm sorry

If I could go back, do it again
I'd be someone you could call friend
Please, please believe that I'm sorry
Please, please believe that I'm sorry

ALICE PUNG

Alice is a writer, editor, teacher and lawyer based in Melbourne. Born a month after her Chinese parents fled from Cambodia to Australia as asylum seekers from Pol Pot's Khmer Rouge Regime, Alice has used her shared family's experiences to write stories that captivate all readers.

She has won numerous awards including 2007 Newcomer of the Year Award, Australia Book Industry Awards for her first book *Unpolished Gem*. *Her Father's Daughter*, the book where the short story *The Bus* came from, won the Western Australia Premier's Book Award for Non Fiction, and was shortlisted for the Premier's Literary Awards in Victoria and New South Wales, and nominated in the Queensland Literary Awards. *Laurinda* was published in 2014 and she is writing four books around the character Marly for Penguin's *Our Australian Girl* series.

THE BUS

DAUGHTER–

It was when she was sick that she first realised her father would do anything for her. She must have been about five. She woke up in the middle of the night, and he made her jam on toast. Then, when she had heavy asthma at eleven and was housebound for two weeks, he bought her ice cream, the expensive kind, with real strawberries in it. But when she was really little, about four, she had the flu and had some idea about death. She whimpered on the couch and said, 'Dad, I don't want to die.'

'Be quiet and drink this Milo,' he told her, rubbing Vicks Vaporub on her chest.

Her father, she noticed as she grew older, never used the words death or die, unlike her mum and grandmother and aunties. If they dropped something, it was 'Si oh!' *Go die*. If they made a mistake. If they heard some bad news, such as their child getting less than ninety per cent in an exam. But her father never uttered it.

There were some things they would never mention again, like the box-cutter boy. And other things which he didn't mind her finding out. 'If you want to know about the time of Pol Pot, I will introduce you to people,' her father told her a year after the box-cutting incident, 'and they will talk to you and tell you about their lives.'

He took her to visit his friends in suburban houses with neat front yards in Footscray and Springvale, and they would tell her tales of survival. She remembered these moments, how at some pivotal point these older folk began to speak to her as if they no longer saw her as a child but as someone who would store these stories, and who might one day convey them to their own progeny, who were too preoccupied with building houses and bringing up babies to sit and listen.

There they both were, she and her father, sitting on a couch in a strange man's house. The man, a friend of her father, was a furniture-maker. He had made the couch himself. She looked at him, and then looked back down at the couch. How could a man as thin as that make a thing of wood and leather as robust as the sofa set they were all sitting on? She realised her father and she sat in the exact same way. They perched on their tailbones at the very edge of the seat, as if to sink back and get comfortable would be to indulge themselves.

Perhaps this story was not meant to begin on a bus in China at all.

Perhaps it was meant to begin on another bus, in another place, during another time.

The bus, the man said. It loaded us on, and then took us to the top of a mountain and dumped us there. The mountain was dotted with landmines. At the top there was no food or water, so we went down and exploded and died.

But the man was sitting in front of them, telling this story, so obviously he had not died. Neither had his wife, who was serving them cups of tea. Chinese cups were very small, she realised. You could not hug them in your hands and lean back on a couch, ready for a yarn. The size of a cup was probably the measure of a society's loquaciousness. You couldn't tell a long-winded story about a visit to the supermarket while holding a Chinese cup with two fingers. Its contents were two gulps. The end. So your story needed significance, but not the kind of tall-poppy significance that would upstage your friend. One thing those who came from Cambodia were good at doing was keeping quiet, and listening. Another thing was telling a story using the most direct route, like that bus carrying those people she would never meet. Depositing them like a dumpster at the precipice of a very high tip. Who was the first at the top of the mountain to start worrying, she wondered, and the first to make their way down?

She may never know what happened, but perhaps it was time for her to take a stab in the dark.

ARWA ABOUSAMRA

Arwa is a Palestinian-Australian author born in Saudi Arabia. A mother of three and an Arabic interpreter, she has written for SBS food magazine *Feast*, *The Sunday Telegraph* and released her memoir *Tea with Arwa* in 2011. *Muslim Footprint* was first published in the anthology *Coming of Age*.

Arwa continues to write and has recently completed a Masters degree in interpreting and translation at Western Sydney University and is a qualified Arabic interpreter.

MUSLIM FOOTPRINT

The first time I set foot on Australian land it was 1985 and I was nearly nine years old. The flight seemed to go on forever, and once we were on the ground we were *literally* on the other side of the world. My heart skipped a beat as the aeroplane touched down at Kingsford Smith Airport. I didn't know a lot about Australia then – I didn't know who Kingsford Smith was, or that Vegemite existed; to me Australia was the land of kangaroos and koalas. I knew it was a long way from Saudi Arabia, the land where I was born that wouldn't recognise my citizenship. We were coming to this vast new country because my mother and father wanted their children to have a place to call home.

We landed in the early hours of the morning and despite my exhaustion my body buzzed with anticipation from being in this new country. I wanted to get our bags and get out of the air-conditioned terminal so I could breathe this strange new air. We were greeted by my mother's younger brother, Mohammad. Uncle Mohammad had lived in Liverpool, a suburb in Sydney, for many years and had helped my parents to make the huge decision to move their family to Australia.

Even though I was born in Riyadh, the capital of Saudi Arabia, I wasn't Saudi Arabian. I was a third-generation Palestinian who'd never seen Palestine because of the Israeli invasion in 1948. This invasion has caused the displacement of over five million Palestinians in the past 60 years, and many deaths.

Despite my not being able to call myself a child of that country, Saudi Arabia was 'home' for me.

I loved everything about the Saudi desert terrain: the palm trees everywhere you looked; the smell of the fragrant, dry air; the fine, powder-like sand that swirled around in mini-tornadoes as the desert wind swept through the city. No matter how tightly my mother shut the windows against the elements, sand still managed to get into our home. It drove her crazy.

The eloquently beautiful call to prayer that echoed through the city five times a day always lifted my spirit. Saudi Arabia is the birthplace of the Prophet Mohammad (peace be upon him), and home of the holy cities of Mecca and Medina that I visited as a child and that hold a dear place in my heart. Seeing the Kaaba, the sacred stone that is cherished by all Muslims, was a magnificent sight, as are the black covers that bear verses from the holy Quran embroidered in golden thread.

None of us had seen Uncle Mohammad for many years, and my younger brother had never met him. It was a meeting full of hugs and tears. We didn't all fit in my uncle's car, so Dad, my sister Reem and I went by cab. By then the sun had risen and Sydney was coming to life; people were on their way to work and kids were walking to school. I watched it all and my breath caught when I saw schoolgirls wearing uniforms that were above their knees. And they were walking with boys. Some were even holding hands! I was wide-eyed and blushing. In Saudi Arabia our uniforms had been ankle-length and all the schools were segregated.

Seeing those girls with their short uniforms made me uneasy. Was I going to have to dress like them? Modest dress was a part of our life back in Saudi Arabia. I wasn't old enough to wear my hijab yet, but my two older sisters were. My mother, who wore the hijab in Saudi Arabia, made the very personal and difficult decision that she and my sisters would not wear it when we moved to Australia. My parents were concerned we would not be accepted if we were so noticeably different. They did not know if people would mistreat us or turn their back on us because of the way we dressed. I couldn't imagine such a thing. Not then.

I was a child of many worlds who didn't feel quite right in any.

Our first visit to Australia lasted a year. We lived in Grafton before moving back to Saudi Arabia in 1986. No one in Grafton knew where Palestine was. Every time someone asked me where I was from and I'd say 'Palestine', they would say 'Pakistan?'. I would have to show them Palestine on a map. This was amazing to me; I'd heard songs during Christmas mentioning Bethlehem and Bethlehem was in Palestine, so why did so many not know where it was? What was the missing link?

In 1989 we moved back to Australia, this time to the Sydney suburb of Liverpool, and even in two years things had changed. There were now visibly more cultures around, and especially Muslim ones. I was a little different too. I was nearly twelve and had finished Year 6 back in Saudi Arabia, where I wore my hijab to school. When we arrived back in Australia, my mother again decided that we shouldn't wear it.

My first day of high school was nerve-racking. I was excited and frightened at the same time. My anxiety was multiplied by a million because I wasn't just starting a new school, I was starting again in a new country.

I wondered if there were going to be girls like me from the Middle East. Would there be any Muslim students in my class? And how many of them would have just arrived in Australia as I had? Would they speak Arabic like me? Would I be able to keep up with the schoolwork? Would I make friends?

As I walked through the school gates I was so anxious I thought my heart would stop. I felt bare not wearing my hijab and an ankle-length uniform. My uniform was two sizes too big so it would cover my knees, but I still felt self-conscious. My sisters felt the same way. We all felt lost. Having sisters at school made little difference to me, they were in different grades and I was going to be all alone.

Despite my anxiety, I tried to smile as much as I could. I always believed a smile could crumble the toughest heart; if someone smiled at you, natural instinct would make you smile back. So despite shaky legs and a thousand-mile-a-minute heartbeat, I smiled at every student who walked by. Some smiled back and even looked as nervous as I did, but others ignored me and walked straight by. I guess they were all worried about being in high school.

I wanted to make friends and belong so badly that I was drawn to a group of girls who were Arab like me. Liverpool Girls High School in 1990 had a small number of Muslim students spread out across the years; some were in Year 7 with me, and others in Year 9 and 10 or higher. They were from various Middle Eastern backgrounds. Some had a Lebanese background, others were from Jordan. Age differences didn't matter, as we formed a bond due to being children of migrant parents.

The girls spoke Arabic and English with Australian accents as most of them had been born in Australia and called themselves Arabs. At lunch they ate Arab bread rolls filled with labna and olives, zatar (herbs, sesame, salt) and cheese. They spoke Arabic and looked Arab. Most of them had long uniforms like me and others wore tights underneath to cover their legs. They reminded me of my friends back in Saudi Arabia. But I soon found out that we were very different. We shared a connection on the outside, but the more I got to know them the more I found that was all we had in common. These Arab girls were unsettled and they fought with the Australian girls. They felt like outsiders in their own country and lashed out because of it. The Aussie girls teased and made fun of the Muslim girls during Ramadan. They walked by and threw water at us and called us stupid for not eating or drinking water all day. They found it easy to make fun of something they didn't understand.

They called us 'filthy Arabs' or 'wogs', and told us all to go back to our own country. Because we looked different, it was easy to label us. We were bound by a culture that was misunderstood by most and a religion that was unknown to many. I didn't like aggression and anger, so I held my tongue and kept out of the way.

I was always a proud and passionate student who loved school. Arabic language and grammar were my strengths, but in Australia I struggled. I was scared of being called stupid because I couldn't read and write as well as the other students. I could speak English very well and even had a prominent American accent due to some time spent in the United States when I was three. But my reading and writing skills were at a beginner's level. I struggled with the simplest words.

It was frustrating because up until then I had been one of the top students in all my classes. In Australia I felt a heaviness in my heart. I did not want to draw attention to myself and avoided reading out loud in class. I changed my seat so it would never be my turn, or asked the teacher if I could be excused to go to the toilet. It was exhausting and all-consuming to be constantly thinking of escape.

Once my Year 8 teacher was in a terrible mood and she refused to let me out of the classroom. There was no escape this time. There was a stabbing pain in my chest as though I was out of breath and drowning. It was my turn to read next. I was sweating and shaking, and it seemed that the paragraph was endless. I made mistakes with words I knew and the teacher corrected me, but I was deaf to what she was saying. The other students' snickering and laughing was too loud. This was one of the many anxiety attacks I experienced during my learning years.

In a maths class we were shown some problems that I had learned in Year 6 in Saudi Arabia. I knew the answers, but I couldn't write on paper as well as I could talk. And some things were just lost in translation. I felt trapped. I looked at the teacher with wide eyes and used all the words I knew to explain how to solve the equation, feeling that I was facing the world with one arm tied behind my back. I was always playing catch-up. Homework took twice as long; I needed to look up every second word in the dictionary.

With all the struggles in my learning, and the conflict I saw in the playground, I am surprised I stayed as happy as I did. But my sisters and my family gave me strength, and my spirit meant I would keep looking for a way to connect to Australia. All I needed was a footprint of some sort to follow, but there was nothing. Muslims were absent in all I was learning about the world. No subject or topic at school mentioned Islam. It is still largely absent in the school curriculum. I couldn't understand it then, or now. But one day I discovered 'the Afghan cameleers', who were early Muslim pioneers and played an integral part in the discovery of outback Australia. Many settlements wouldn't have been possible without them.

The Afghani cameleers, along with their camels, were invited to Australia by colonial settlers to assist in the discovery of the outback territories. With limited water supplies, the early settlers had struggled making the journey across the outback. The camel, the ship of the desert, was the only answer. Finally, here was a footprint in the sand of outback Australia. Here were stories of Muslims who had done many good things and whom I shared something with – a religion, and also a love of this new place, Australia.

After three years of high school I met my first veiled Muslim friend in Australia. Abbey and her family had moved from Kuwait, and her father was Palestinian too. We connected instantly and I moved away from the angry Arab girls. She and I shared stories of growing up in the Middle East, and bonded over our love for the countries we came from.

Abbey was funny and energetic and she put a smile on anyone's face, but these qualities didn't matter when we stepped outside school and faced the real world. People only saw her as a young girl wearing a hijab, and the looks she got were anything but kind.

Walking through the shops in Liverpool with her, I noticed how she got the dirtiest looks. These people didn't know Abbey and yet they had no hesitation in judging her because of her hijab. After one such walk I was so bothered by how many people were looking at her in an unkind way that I asked, 'Doesn't it bother you?' She said, 'You get used to it after a while.' This made me very angry.

I wondered many times how Abbey could be so strong and confident in wearing her hijab, even though she was one of a few who wore it at school or in the local community of Liverpool. She told me she had decided one day that she was not going to worry about pleasing anyone but Allah, and thus made the decision to put her hijab on and face the world happy with who she was.

I was impressed with Abbey, but these experiences deterred me from ever considering wearing the hijab as a teenager. I wasn't strong enough to face a society that would judge me because of what I was wearing without knowing me. Not then. It would be seven years before I found the courage to wear the hijab. To face the world as a visible Muslim took some self-education. But after I decided to put it on, I wondered how I had ever left home without it. Now it is a part of me, an extension of my being that I will never forfeit again.

I went on finding my way in school, with Abbey by my side, I slowly became more confident in my schoolwork and learned how to read and write better through the years. My spelling in English has never been perfect but I don't feel shame any more. I just make a note to myself and practise, practise, practise.

My friendship with Abbey encouraged my faith. We talked about religion and shared what we knew about Islam. I was praying more regularly even at school. Abbey and I asked teachers for permission to use a classroom at lunchtime for our midday prayer. It only took five minutes and every time we used a different room.

Sometimes the teachers would say no as they didn't understand why we couldn't use a quiet, clean spot in the playground to do it. They had no idea what a Muslim prayer looked like, no idea that we wash beforehand and prostrate ourselves on the ground. So we snuck into empty classrooms and prayed in a rush.

A few times we were caught and the teacher was

understanding, after we explained that we were just praying and needed to be in a quiet place; but there were those who didn't want to hear about it. Once we were caught by a teacher while we were in the middle of our prayer. She didn't understand that we weren't being rude in not answering her when she called out to us. When we finished we explained that we couldn't interrupt our prayer to respond to her. She was not sympathetic. She asked us not to use her room and made us pick up rubbish from the playground as a punishment.

I wanted to be part of changing things around me, of encouraging acceptance and understanding, especially in school. I decided to try my luck at becoming a prefect at the end of Year 11. I was worried about what the outcome would be, but to my surprise the teachers and students voted me in. It was a very proud moment for me and my parents were very happy too. For them it was a sign that their daughter was finding her home and sense of self.

I was also elected to be a member of the student council and so was Abbey, and it gave me a chance to suggest to the school that Muslim students should have a place where they could pray during lunchtime.

The principal agreed. At first it was a small group, but as the news spread, more started to join in. By that time there were Muslim girls from many different backgrounds. Pakistanis and Indians, Bosnians and even some of my old Arab friends joined in. I remember a few of the Aussie girls noticing that we were coming to a classroom every lunchtime and finally they asked me one day, 'What do you guys do in there?' I invited them in to show them what Muslim prayer looks like, and they were very intrigued.

That was one of the proudest moments of my high-school years. I had made a difference and I was able to help demystify Islam and what Muslims do. It gave me hope: a hope that if you put your mind to something, you can make a difference. I made a footprint of my own; it may have been a small one, but it mattered to me and other Muslim students at Liverpool Girls High School. I hope that it turned something that seemed different into something normal. And perhaps the next Muslim Australian girl who started school the year I left never felt she didn't belong. She had a footprint to follow.

Felicity's latest book is *The Incredible Here and Now* (Giramondo, 2013), which has won the Prime Minister's Literature Award (YA) and been shortlisted for the New South Wales Premier's Literature Awards, the Western Australian Premier's Book Awards and The Children's Book Council of Australia Book of the Year Award. Her work has been produced for radio and television as well as being featured in many newspapers and journals.

She likes writing and teaching and boxing and hanging out with her son. You can find out more about her at felicitycastagna.net

THE GIRLS

So. This is how it goes. Summer. We spend the longest, longest time getting ready on the nights when Mum works night shift and Asheeka comes over and we watch the street and plan our moves and talk about the boys and Asheeka uses her eyeliner pen to make my eyes pop out like two round pieces of fruit cake.

Right now we're hanging over the balcony in Mum's old bathrobes like we're in some five-star hotel in the movies. Like we're celebrities and all that, waiting for our fans to show up and wave and hold up signs. *I love you Rosa, I love you Asheeka,* those signs would say but no, not today. Today there's only the red flashes of lights from a police car parked up the street and the sun setting through the spaces between the apartment blocks, spreading itself across the road like some kind of golden slime. It's still so hot in the night-time that everyone's sitting on plastic chairs on nobody's lawn outside the apartment blocks. People just hanging with their phones on speaker so you can hear their music.

Asheeka leans against the railing, unfolds her hands, lights a cigarette she stole from her dad's pack. She looks bored. She always looks bored when things make her nervous. She's wearing one of those skirts and tops where the top isn't long enough so there's this space where you show off your belly. That's what's in now so she'll wear it every day even if it's too cold to be showing off your body parts until something else's in.

I was getting myself done up when she arrived at my apartment door, her black eyeliner smudged, her hair in a messy bun on the top of her head. I know when she's like this, when everything's not the glamour it should be that there's something wrong. These days the something wrong is usually Arnold and his boys – the ones we're hooking up with later tonight.

Down on the street, my upstairs neighbour is standing in Nikes that flash small red lights every time he leans a slightly different way against his mate's new lowered Honda. All his friends are inside, he's on the outside. No one is moving. They're just scheming to do something later. That's it, that's what everyone does here. Cars. Cars. Cars – driving around, leaning against them, looking good. Looking excellent. Showing off your muscles or your leopard-print dress.

I realise the dress I'm wearing isn't even zipped up at the back. Asheeka gave me this dress after our last fight. When I tried it on, she said the same thing she always says, *Looks good, you need a fake tan, but. Buy it in a can at Chemist Warehouse and I can put it on ya.* I look at Asheeka and I look at my dress and I try to zip it up but the zipper gets stuck. 'I don't know,' I say. 'Maybe something else. I don't know if I can walk down the street in those heels and this dress. And you know everyone in their cars is gonna honk at me and there's that guy on the corner who tries it on every time and also, maybe my relatives or something, maybe they'll tell my mum.'

Asheeka puts her middle finger up and says, 'That's what you do to all of them.' But I can't do that stuff right. Not like Asheeka does, not with that same kind of look that says I am totally absolutely sure of everything I'm doing.

Ash falls from her cigarette to the floor of the balcony. She's not even smoking. It's disgusting, everyone knows it, but sometimes it's part of the look. When I'm closer to her I can see that her mascara isn't really smudged. It's some kinda bruise. A black eye. I know black eyes because Asheeka was the first person to give me one. I covered for her but – that's what you do. She punched me in the eye with that big ring of hers because I told her that she was too good for Arnold and his crew. Some girls, they just love the wrong kinda guys. I thought about it later, and I understood that he'd hurt her and she'd hurt me, not that that's all right, but just that's how it is. We got hauled into the principal's office, the two of us sitting there, me with my black eye. I remember how Principal Alloshi looked at her like he was suspicious and said, 'Juanita, what happened?' He called her Juanita approximately half the time because Asheeka and Juanita were the only black students in our year at school and he couldn't tell them apart. I don't know why she never corrected him. That time, she just shrugged her shoulders and looked at the floor, and I said *I fell down the stairs*.

I can't remember what Arnold had done to her that time. Truth is, I've always been jealous of her. She just carries it. You know? Like she owns the world or something and everyone believes her. Everyone except Arnold.

The Hare Krishnas in the last house on the corner start their drumming and someone turns up Eminen so they don't have to hear it.

'You know,' Asheeka says, 'we should get going. Everyone'll be waiting.'

I leave her on the balcony to change in the other

room. In the wardrobe mirror I check myself out. I wish I had curves, I wish I had a lot of things, a bit more height maybe. I check the red and blond streaks in my hair. Asheeka told me how to do them from a packet you buy at Priceline. She told me I needed them and that I also needed to learn to use those wax strips to do my eyebrows and that I also needed to paint my nails in red at least once every couple of weeks. She said everyone would respect me more if I did these things. She said it like it was a fact. And it was.

When I'm changed things move quickly. The streets suck us in again and we're walking down Church Street towards Guildford/Merrylands way when we see the sign emerging – that yellow, yellow glow of the McDonald's 'M'. In two years, when we're eighteen, we'll go clubbing in the city or at least to the local pub, but for now, this is where it's at on a Friday night – in the car park of course – no one hangs inside.

We pass the last apartment block at the end of my street and Asheeka has gone ahead. She has these muscles on the back of her lower legs. I don't get where she got those from or the swimmer's shoulders. I can see the red soles on her heels as we hit the lights coming out of the restaurants on Church Street. *That's how you know they're not Kmart crap*, she told me once, *because the leather is underneath the shoe, not just on top*. She's the only sixteen-year-old I know that doesn't shop at Supre. Most of her clothes are like this, bought with three evenings a week of putting the clothes people leave on the Myer dressing room floor back in their place.

We stop on the corner where the Fijian-Indians used to sell cooked yams. Now there's the bright lights of a brand-new Coles. Everything is changing. We go left, past the emo pub and the Croatian bakery near the station and we head under the overpass. Asheeka asks me random life questions whenever the street goes quiet and I know it's because she can't stand the silent spaces. The housos that Asheeka lived in when we first started high school used to be somewhere around here. It's dark and she holds my hand as she scans the street. She thinks I might get easily distracted and wander off like I used to when we were in Year Seven. She likes to keep me close to her so that she knows I am safe.

When we get to McDonald's Arnold and his crew are all leaning up against his car. He's wearing saggy jeans and a 59Fifty cap even though it's dark. He's not that much bigger than Asheeka, but he stands there like he's huge. Only two months since he's had this old Ford Falcon. Painted it with the blue house paint he found in his parents' shed and made it shiny with discount wood lacquer from Bunnings. He's got new seat covers in a dark red. Not too bad looking. It's his everything and he doesn't let many people inside it, except Asheeka.

Tonight he's just hanging back, watching the Filipino kids breakdance. He knows we're here but he doesn't say nothing. Neither does Asheeka. When Kylie and Paul and Steve and Ellie from school come over to say hi, Asheeka gets up all close to Paul. Everyone's talking about how Mr Alloshi kicked two kids out of school the other day but I know that Asheeka's not paying attention to it. She's got her head snuggled up against Paul's shoulder and she's looking out at Arnold like she's trying to get his attention.

There's kids taking up every bit of the car park, just hanging, talking to their friends, strutting their stuff. The security guy's got his arms crossed. He's looking at everyone like he's gonna start a rumble but we all know he won't. Above there's this big white moon behind the McDonald's 'M' and it's like every bit of everywhere is lit up. I'm staring at that moon, not noticing much when Arnold comes over and yanks Asheeka hard by the arm and silently drags her over to his car where he throws her in the passenger seat and slams the car door. No one says nothing.

I just watch the place for a while. Sometimes I hate this, the way that stuff just happens and everyone goes silent. Paul and Steve and Kylie and Ellie keep on talking about those two kids, and Arnold is leaning against the back of his car like he's got his dog back in its big blue cage. So I walk on over there and press my fingers to the windscreen of the car and Asheeka's in there, arms crossed, looking like she's filled with a rage so big she could crack the windscreen with it. When I tap the window with my nails again, she opens the door and whispers, 'Get in.'

I do like she says and Asheeka squishes over to the driver's seat and I notice that Arnold's keys are just sitting there in the ignition. 'Sometimes', I say because I don't know what else to say, 'it sucks being a girl.'

And she thinks about it for a while and turns the ignition and says, 'Maybe it doesn't always have to suck.'

As soon as the engine starts to whizz Arnold starts yelling from the outside and Asheeka presses the button that makes all the doors lock. She turns to me and grabs my hand and squeezes it a little and says, 'We could go anywhere.'

'Anywhere.'

'Like movie stars,' she says.

'Us in our big fancy car. Just cruising without the boys.'

'Better that way.'

Asheeka puts the car in reverse and taps her foot down on the pedal. She's got one hand on the wheel and the other's holding mine, and I look up into that big fat moon and I almost can't hear Arnold screaming.

GAYLE KENNEDY

Gayle is a member of the Wongaibon clan of south-west New South Wales. She was Indigenous Issues editor/writer for *Streetwize Comics* from 1995-1998. She has published 11 children's books with Oxford University Press, and in 2006 her book *Me, Antman & Fleabag* won the Queensland Premier's Literary Awards, David Unaipon Award, and was shortlisted for the Victorian Premier's Literary Award and Deadly Award. She has had articles, poetry and short stories published in publications as diverse as *The Australian Women's Weekly*, *Reader's Digest*, *The Sydney Morning Herald*, *Edinburgh Review* and *Ora Nui*.

KOORI GIRL GOES SHOPPIN'

We're all the same under the skin dear
Said the lady at the bus stop
Outta the blue, for no reason
Cos I was just sittin' there
Waitin' on the 433

Get back to Redfern ya black slag
Yelled the kids in the hotted up Torana
Outta the blue, for no reason
Cos I was just window shoppin'
And thinking 'bout Saturday night

You gunna buy that CD young lady?
Growled the security guard
Outta the blue, for no reason
Cos I was just lookin' for a present for me cuz
And she likes hip hop and rap and stuff

Why the long lip bub?
Asked my mother
Outta the blue, for no reason
Cos I was just sittin' there
Watchin' *Home and Away*
And thinking bout how I went shoppin'
And came home with nothing

DAVINA BELL

Davina is the author of the Alice books in the *Our Australian Girl* series, which follow the story of a young ballerina growing up in World War One, as well as picture books for younger readers.

She worked at Penguin for six years as an editor, and now lives in the Margaret River region of Western Australia's south-west, where she writes full time on the edge of a vineyard. *A Thousand Silver Ghosts* is based on an extract from her latest project, a young adult novel. She has previously been published in *Best Australian Stories* 2007 and 2008.

A THOUSAND SILVER GHOSTS

It was a blue whale. Yes, I know they're not, like, common, but even in the moonlight it was kind of hard to mistake the largest mammal that ever lived. He was washed up where the shoreline used to be because the tide had gone out so far it was touching yesterday, and I kid you not, that whale was as long as a car-park traffic jam after a game of football.

I went and sat next to his eye, that big old guy – plopped myself down next to it on the sand and leant back. I knew that even if I chugged all the condensed milk I had with me, I wouldn't be able to lift so much as a flipper to save him – his barnacles alone were the size of my head. And BTW if you think it's sexist that I automatically assumed he was a boy, well, I didn't; he told me later.

'Have we *both* got problems,' I said to him, rustling around in my backpack for a can of milk and yanking at the ring of its lid. 'You're clearly not going anywhere in a hurry, and boy am I ever mad at my brother.'

'I had a brother once,' he said thoughtfully. 'Got eaten by an orca. Everyone thinks they're so cute but they're vicious little sons of bitches.'

'You're telling me. Don't I know all about people who come across so gentle, then – BOOM! They blow your heart into tatters. Want any of this?'

'If you wouldn't mind sharing, kid.'

I cracked open another tin and poured the whole thing onto his tongue and spread it around, because neither of us was quite sure where his taste receptors were. In the end I think he got the general flavour profile and he seemed to enjoy it. And then I did some handsprings and cartwheels on the sand to keep warm – basic stuff really, but he was impressed, and it was nice to have an audience after being ignored for so long.

'So your brother,' he said, 'he has legs, I presume. He can do all this, too?'

'Even better,' I admitted, remembering how Teddy used to shimmy up to the tree house.

'Maybe not any more, though, because his legs are like toothpicks.'

'Marathon running?' asked the whale. 'The professional circuit?'

'Nah. Stopped eating,' I said.

'Anorexia,' the whale said, nodding. Yes, I get that he didn't have an articulated neck so it wasn't technically nodding, but that was definitely his vibe. 'Body image. Much more of a thing for boys than you'd think.'

'I'm not even sure if it's that, exactly,' I said, though I'd read the diagnosis on the charts, heard it around the hospital. 'I mean, sure it is, but the whole thing has a context.'

'My name's Mikie, by the way,' said the whale. 'Why don't you start at the beginning? I think I have time to hear it from there.'

And to tell you the truth, this guy had nothing *but* time, and I would have felt sorry for him if he wasn't so magnificent that he was beyond pity. So I introduced myself properly and sat back down and started from the beginning, which was me and Teddy bumping up against each other in our his-and-hers amniotic sacs. How it felt to be a twin when you're not with your twin, like a cut-up apple, raw and half.

I told him about our father dying, and our mother, the famous writer, and our tree house up so high that nobody's parents would let them climb it. I told him about being dyslexic, and how when Teddy played our dad's old banjo, I was so good at singing harmonies that we could have started a family band. 'This story has a point,' I assured the whale as I ran my finger along the inside of the can. 'I'm getting there.'

'Oh, I'm enjoying it,' said Mikie. 'Don't leave out anything on my account.'

I told him about the boy up the road, who I'd loved since before I even knew I had a heart. How it was him and Teddy and me, us three always. How each year I put the star on the top of the Christmas tree by standing up tall, one foot on each of their shoulders. How wherever he was in the neighbourhood, I could feel him, that boy; how I knew where he was, like we were joined by a lasso made of light.

'Handsome chap?' said Mikie.

'Do you know who Ryan Gosling is?' I asked the whale. It was a long shot, but then again he seemed to know a lot of things.

'As if I wouldn't. Dreamboat,' said Mikie.

'Totally,' I agreed. 'Well, picture him when he was fifteen wearing a stripy blazer and reading. That was Oscar.'

'Good grief,' said Mikie.

'You bet. You should have seen him in skinny jeans. He came with us to France for a whole summer – the European summer, I mean. My mother rented a house there. She had to finish her latest book. Our school said no, but she took us anyway. Oscar too. His parents let him. They loved my mother. She and Oscar could have talked about books all night. They did once, actually.'

'Always wanted to see the Mediterranean,' said Mikie, wistfully.

'Maybe in your next life,' I said, and then wished I hadn't, because do dying people want to be reminded or do they want to forget? 'Anyway,' I said quickly, 'we were there for three months. I mean, we were supposed to be. Is this boring for you?' I asked, because I've been told I can get carried away with the romance of my own narrative, and a beach in the moonlight is just the sort of place that can happen if you're predisposed.

'I'll tell you if it's starting to lag,' Mikie assured me. 'You sure have an eye for detail, kid.'

So I told him how my mother wrote under a tree in the villa's stony shade, and it was us three loose in the endless summer. How it felt to lie each morning with our stomachs on the hot stones, slick from the pool and breathing hard. How I got stung by a bee in a lavender field and Oscar pulled it out with his teeth, that sting, his lips just above the fold of my knee. I told him about eating peaches still warm from the trees, and pushing each other in a wheelbarrow through the hazy olive groves, never a shoe between us.

How we poured pink wine into tumblers and held them up to the sunset, all winking, crystal love.

'Very European,' Mikie said approvingly. 'Discourages binge drinking later on.'

I told him about nights on the tiny sailboat, crisp in the starlight; how none of us talked as we flew over the sea. How it clinked against its chains, that little boat, as we tied it up at dawn.

'And then what happened?'

I gazed out at the sand, miles of it, glowing like opals under the moon.

'They fell in love,' I said eventually. 'Or maybe they were in love the whole time and I hadn't noticed.'

'Teddy and Oscar?' Mikie asked gently.

I swallowed. 'Yep.'

'A question, kid,' said the whale. 'Just to make sure. I get the whole gay thing. But are you meaning romantic love, or platonic?'

I remembered their hands by the pool at midnight.

I remembered sitting up in the bell tower, seeing them down in the meadow throwing grapes into each other's mouths, heads tilted up to the sun.

I remembered how they kissed up in the hayloft and their lips fizzed stars. I'd seen them through the high little window where you could watch the moon rise, my heartbeat strong in my ears as the world fell down.

I swallowed. 'Romantic,' I said.

'What did you do?' asked Mikie.

'I sulked,' I admitted. 'Hid away and cried a lot. I did heaps of – what do you call it? Glowering. My mother based a really awful character in her novel on me. Said she was the best villain she'd ever come up with.' I chewed on my lip a little. 'I loved him so much that I just assumed . . .'

'Wouldn't be too rough on yourself, kid. All love has risks,' said Mikie. 'All love is opening up your clamshell for someone else to rummage about in. That's what it is to be alive.'

'Dumb,' I said.

'Might seem so now. But you're still young. With a longer future ahead of you than I have, filled with the chance to love and be loved. Isn't that something?'

Mikie seemed kind of tired, and I wondered if I'd worn him out. And then it hit me that perhaps it wasn't me that had worn him out. Perhaps he was dying. 'Oh gosh – shouldn't I be keeping you wet, like they do on the news? Spraying you with a hose or something? I'm so sorry – I sat here jabbering and let you dry out.'

'No need to hose me down, kid. We both know it's too late for that. Just tell me how it all ended up.'

'Are you sure?' I asked him, hugging my knees. 'Because it gets pretty sad.'

'I figured,' said Mikie. 'You're here, aren't you?'

I looked around at The End of the World and I nodded. 'Well, one night, a hot night, they went out to the hayloft. Teddy said they couldn't sleep in their room – too stuffy. They took a candle out there. They climbed onto the platform with the little high-up window where you could see the moon.'

I looked up at Mikie to see if he was following the subtext and boy, was his big eye gorgeous.

'It caught fire as they were sleeping, the whole thing just one solid wall of flame. And Teddy, he got out – broke through that little high-up window, all in a panic. Cracked it with the blunt of his elbow and dived out through the shards. What do you call it? Fight or flight.'

Months later, I'd walked in on him changing, a T-shirt half over his head, and I saw the bites from that window. There were other things, too – a fresh wound, big and ripe as a pear, that made me cry out and Teddy turn around and slam the door.

But I'd already seen it all by then: the row of slashes on his chest like frozen lightning, his hip bones, so much of them, his prison-bar ribs. I screamed through the door: *You PROMISED. You PROMISED ME, Teddy.* But he didn't say anything back.

'And Oscar?' prodded Mikie.

I shook my head because I couldn't say it, even after a year.

'Oh, kid,' said the whale.

My mother had written so much in that year since we brought Oscar home in plastic and calico. She had written him into a book on wind farms, but Teddy had found him there, and in a dotcom thriller, and a children's book about adventure-seeking mice. She had written Oscar as a crane, as the sun, as the softness of thread. And each time Teddy had found him in her words, and howled, and she'd promised never again.

But she couldn't keep her promise, and Teddy couldn't keep his, not any of them, and I couldn't keep living among the ashes of all those promises, and that's how I'd ended up here, at The End of the World, where there isn't any hope.

'I wish there was something I could say,' said Mikie. 'That poor boy.'

'They said he died quickly,' I whispered. 'That he didn't suffer.'

'I mean your brother,' said Mikie. A tear slipped down from his eye and it was so big that, I kid you not, it was like a bucket of warm water being tipped over my head.

Then we didn't say anything, not for ages, because I hate having wet hair when it's chilly, and I was mad at Teddy for choosing Oscar's ghost and giving up, instead of a life with me. The last thing I wanted was someone feeling sorry for him when I'd been carrying him around in my guts like a dead star. It struck me right then that, boy, I was tired.

'Kid?' the whale whispered through my nap haze, who knows how much later.

'Yes, Mikie?'

'If it isn't too much trouble, will you stay with me?' said the whale. 'Until the end? It won't be much longer.'

'It would be an honour,' I said, because it wasn't his fault, not a single bit of it, and if there's one thing we all wished, it was that Oscar hadn't died alone.

I pulled my backpack over and riffled through to see if there was anything else that Mikie might be interested in, and that's where I came across Oscar's copy of *The Outsiders*. I had brought it home from France, along with his toothbrush. Sometimes, late at night when I could hear my mother typing, I would run the bristles of that toothbrush over my lips.

'Do you know anything about gangs – teen gangs?' I asked. 'That's what this book's about. Not the druggy ones. I mean the bratty ones who run around town and think they're so tough.'

'What do you think dolphins are?' said Mikie.

'Show-offs,' I agreed.

So even though it's hard for me with the dyslexia and all, I read it out loud, all the way through, but between you and me, I skimmed the part with the fire in the church. I read about Ponyboy Curtis, that handsome gangster who looked up at the stars and ached for something better. Oscar had loved Ponyboy Curtis, I mean *really* loved him, and in hindsight maybe I should have paid more attention to that.

As I started each chapter, I'd put my head to Mikie's jowl to feel the beat of his heart ('Larger than a Mini Cooper,' he'd told me proudly) and though it wasn't exactly racing to start with, by the time we got to the whole 'stay gold' moment near the end, it was only booming once a minute, max.

'Mikie?' I whispered.

'Mmm?' he said sleepily.

'Just checking,' I said.

I leant back against him, wishing that I could have known him out in the ocean, the sun splashing over his belly as he arched up to the sky. I thought of Teddy's heart, so slow now, too, like the flash of a big old lighthouse. I thought of his berry-blue lips and his skin's white fuzz and the red of my eyes from crying.

'Mikie?' I whispered again.

'Hmm?'

'Aren't I enough to stick around for?' It hurt so much to ask, but I had to know the answer.

For a while Mikie didn't say anything, and I hoped he'd understood that I wasn't talking about him, and I guess it was a leading question, but my instinct was that he could tell it to me straight; that he'd run out of time for the types of sweet nothings that you pull out of fortune cookies.

'Sometimes,' he said slowly, 'for some people, the end of the world is bigger than love. It's too much to live through, their suffering. And that's so hard for us to understand from the outside.'

'But I'm suffering, too,' I said angrily. 'No one remembers that.'

'Oh, I get that. Sure I do. Everyone alone in their tight little igloos of grief, your hearts all torn. And Teddy, well, who can say how that ends? But listen: I don't think this place is for you, kid. You wouldn't still be here, talking to me if it was. You'd be way out there –' he flicked his tail towards the horizon, 'looking for Oscar now.'

Boy did I ever cry then, really cry, but I don't think Mikie minded because my tears were salty and I cupped them in my palms and I climbed up on him, really carefully, and rubbed those tears on the bit that I think was his forehead, and he seemed to like that.

'Mikie? I said as I lay with my back on his big old back. 'How will I ever love anyone again?' And

I wasn't just being dramatic. I felt dry like a husk, like a paper girl.

'Kid,' said Mikie, sleepily. 'You are doing it now.'

And as I looked up at that huge plate of a moon, boy, did I ever chew on that.

'Mikie?' I asked one last time. 'If you see Oscar out there, will you tell him –'

But I'm not sure if he heard what I said next, because the tide was coming in with a huge roar, like the big old sigh of a thousand silver ghosts.

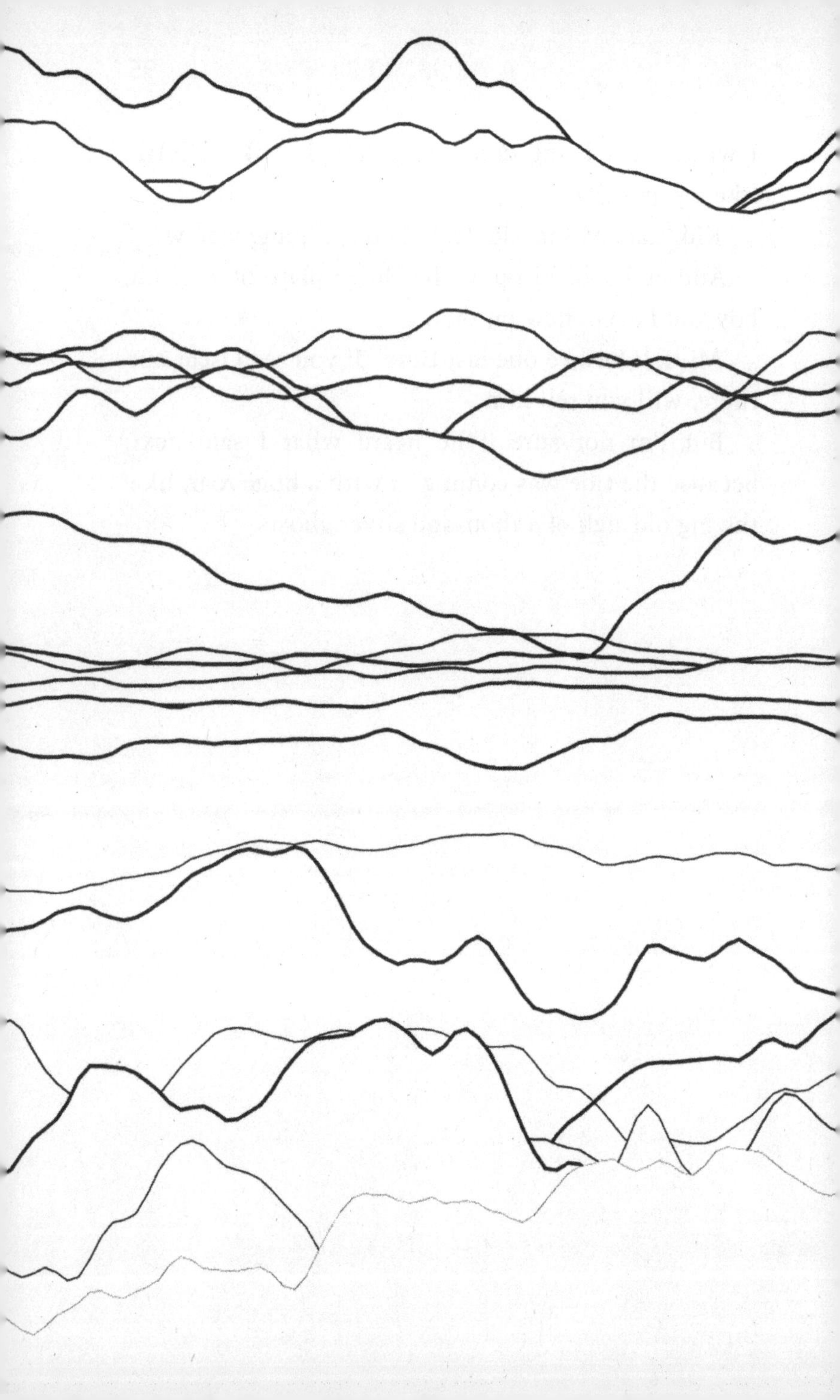

MEG MCKINLAY AND KYLE HUGHES-ODGERS

Meg is an award-winning poet and children's writer. She has published twelve books for children and a collection of poetry for adults. She lives near the ocean in Fremantle, Western Australia, where she dreams up way too many bird metaphors. She still hasn't really accepted that she can't fly.

Kyle is an Australian artist who lives in Perth. He has exhibited artwork and created large-scale public art all over the world. Kyle is also a picture-book creator, and he and Meg McKinlay won the Crystal Kite Award (Australia/New Zealand) for their book *Ten Tiny Things*. Kyle's most recent picture books are *Can a Skeleton Have an X-ray?* and *Off the Wall* (a colouring-in book), both published by Fremantle Press.

HOW TO MAKE A BIRD

To make a bird, you will need a lot of very tiny bones. They will be smaller than you imagine, some so tiny they are barely there. And they will be hollow, these hundreds of bones – so light that when they rest in your palm, you will hardly feel them.

These are what will float on air.

Take these bones and arrange them into a bird-shape. Any bird-shape will do – the proud arch of an eagle, the soft curve of a sparrow.

Breathe deeply, and take your time. The making of a bird is not a thing to be hurried.

Next you need feathers – for warmth and for flight. Smooth these over the bones of your bird-shape, press them firmly into place. Save the longest for the wings and tail; these are what will lift your bird into the air.

Now give your bird, inside its brittle bones, a heart that beats faster than any human heart – a sure, steady heart to carry it across oceans and continents, all the way home at the end of a long winter.

Then add the final touches, like an artist adds her last few brushstrokes, her tiny signature. Give your bird keen eyes for hunting, a beak for building the nest, strong claws for gripping, a song to sing.

Now you have made your bird, with its bones and its feathers and its grasping claws, you might sit back and sigh. You might think to yourself, *I have made this bird . . .*

. . . this silent, still shape of a bird.

But when you see it sitting, cold as a statue, you will know there is more to a bird than all these things you have given it. So you will gather it into your hands and cast it gently upon the air.

Those wings you so carefully made will stretch out just a little, and your bird will tremble as it fills, inside its tiny, racing heart, with the dreams only a bird can dream, of open sky and soaring flight.

And then your bird will catch your eye, and you will know that it is time to open the window.

Set your bird upon the sill and watch while it stretches its wings and looks around with its clear, sharp eyes.

See it shiver as it leans forward onto the air and then takes off in a strong, sudden movement, soaring straight up, away and away, never once looking back . . .

. . . until it is a disappearing speck in a vast blue sky.

And feel your slowly beating heart fill with a kind of sadness, a kind of happiness.

For this is when you will know that you have really made a bird.

MARGO LANAGAN

Margo is an internationally acclaimed author of short stories, novels and poetry. She says: 'I write because it's my way of making sense of the world. I've always loved reading, both to escape from real life and to make life more real, and I like doing both in my writing, too, writing straight realistic and fantasy stories.'

THE QUEEN'S NOTICE

He hurried ahead to the queen-chamber, his jaws aching from the fight. The colony was still reeling from the attack; cousins boiled past and over him with only a quick trace, a chirp or a slight hiss. But he had a mission and a message; they gave way to his shoving, even those larger than he.

The chamber's air was steamy with young. Servers ran about, collecting the ripe young-beads for the compost-chamber. The queen gnawed fresh sweetbulb as the young fought and fixed themselves to her teats. The scent here was absolutely true; it cleared his head of anything but loyalty, and he abased himself. The queen lifted her face from the bulb and sniffed, and gave a trill.

He was dazzled for a moment – then his fellow-fighters jostled from behind, and he remembered his mission. 'It was the sun-start mob,' he panted. 'They came in several ways at once.'

'Dybbol,' came her slow voice. 'I know you.'

'They are gone, sweet queen. You and the young are safe. We blocked all five tunnels that way, and none penetrated.'

'That red-snake last summer. You were the one, weren't you, who turned it back?'

'Among others. We always serve our queen. We always keep the colony.'

'Ha,' she said, and there was more gnawing.

Hunger surfaced in Dybbol's stomach, now that he was no longer saviour. Behind him, some fellow's insides gave a muffled skirl. They were ready to leave.

But the great queen stirred. The young protested, falling off and lolling on the chamber floor. 'Come here, Dybbol,' she said. 'I am all weighed down by our future.'

He pushed the sweetbulb aside and there was her face, warm and curious, her smell piercing his skull like incisors of pure sunlight. Confused, he abased himself and retreated.

Behind him, servers and fighters were twittering. 'Stop your gabble!' the queen shrieked at them, rearing up.

'Bring me food! Attend me, and fast! Come here, Quinnink – I will bat your eyes out for uselessness!'

With his fellow fighters, Dybbol forced a way through the dithering servers. Out in the passage, other smells reached them – pantry was best, and they followed that upward. Hard fighting always made them hungry.

At their head, Dybbol met Amkarra, and made ready to lock teeth with her as always.

But she gave no fight. 'Hunh?' he said. 'Why do you back and abase yourself?' He pursued her down a side-tunnel. Behind him his fellows flowed on towards pantry.

'I serve Her-Madam. I keep the colony,' Amkarra muttered.

'Lock with me! Give me your teeth!'

But she put down her face and would not engage.

'Come at me!' He batted her stupid head.

She muttered into her paws.

'Tell me, then – why be abased?'

'You have Queen's Notice all over you,' she said, and backed further, and somehow turned herself in the narrow space, and fled.

It was true, he did smell, strongly and cleanly of deep earth and queen-favour. His mind was beginning to fill with other things, as a quick-tunnel trickles full of loose earth, but he still had the queen's scent in all his skin-folds, creeping in his mouth-hairs, raw and clear, warm and sweet.

But pantry called, and company, and he went to answer both.

He could not find a good fight. Whenever he closed his jaws on someone, they only lay limp. If he took hold and dragged, no one braced or threw their weight. No one would lock teeth and rock with him; no one would bat him back.

So when the beak-snake came, he heard it a long way off; he raised his head before anyone, and was the first one up the best tunnel and blocking. Dig and dig and dig – he sprayed the hard, smooth snout of the thing with earth as it came on. It bumped against the blocking mound, and he felt a flicker of its tongue as he closed the passage, closed out light and snake. He was all fervour and favour, nose to nose with the queen's enemy; he scraped and tamped, while the others hung back and trilled.

'I must save us alone?' he grunted.

Amkarra came forward, and could not stop abasing herself. 'A true scent breathes from you,' she said. 'You have become too beautiful to fight beside.'

'Bah. Go and report, then.'

'Oh no,' she said, and the others twittered, too. 'Her-Madam will want *you*.'

He knew that. It was new, but it was true. He hurried away, trailing the clean, strange smell of his own bravery.

The young were days livelier, beginning to speak and close their jaws on each other. The queen lay almost as if dead, weak from their constant feeding. Beside her lay a bulb so fresh that Dybbol went straight up and secured a bite of it before he reported.

'Ah. You. Bold one,' murmured the queen. 'What do you bring me?'

'Another victory, queen below us all, heart of all our hearts.' It was his gullet speaking, so grateful for food after fighting.

'Against what?'

'Snake, coming from sun-end as they all do, hot with light and hunger.'

'And the size of it?'

'Bigger than any before, Your-Madam. Stronger than twelve cousins. Only speed saved us.'

The queen gave a purring sigh and raised her head. '*Your* speed, Dybbol?'

'Among others, all our queen.' Dybbol made to leave.

'Linger!' cried the queen. Her breath flew at him, cleansing him of hunger and care, and he was there before her, their muzzles touching, her scent locked bright in his head. Deeper in the chamber her immenseness moved against the spilling pile of young. He knew what to do, knew even though it was new: he must go to the far end of her great spine-arch. A scent was coming from her there, that spiralled higher and sweeter in Dybbol's head than any other ever, a scent that beckoned, that dragged him from her muzzle–

Sharp teeth caught in his haunch and flung him against the wall, knocking all scent from his nose. Servers ran anxiously about; young cheeped and squirmed.

The queen shifted. 'Now is not yet the time,' she breathed.

'The time?' He tried to shake his head clear.

'When these Two-Dozen disperse,' she said, 'that will be your time.' And she pulled the bulb towards her and was gnawing.

He hurried away, dizzy with favour. Near the pantry, he met Barraud, one of the queen's two paramours. Dybbol did not give way as he should; instead, he reared and gaped, roughing the air in his mouth-hairs. Here at last would be a fight! Oh, and he was ready – he was unafraid even of a paramour today! He hissed and went forward–

–and met nothing. He fell to his paws. Barraud was gone off-side, two tunnels along.

'Aargh! Face me! Come at me!'

'I will not,' came Barraud's trilling. 'You are all over favoured and must save yourself for Her Immensity!'

'I am not *so* favoured,' cried Dybbol, pursuing. 'Come, I must put my teeth in something!'

'Not me!' Barraud sped ahead, threading through tunnels, forcing cousins aside. 'I will not fight a favoured one!' came back faintly.

Dybbol began to lose him to the weaving tunnels, to the earth – and to a strong scent of alarm, souring the tunnel-mouths to one side. He veered that way, the scents showing place and activity and size-of-danger on the colony-map in his head – in two places. Two different dangers. He made, fast, for the digging danger, which was farther but greater. A snake would only take one fighter, then would leave; a digger might want several, might dig deep, might uncover the colony's heart.

'We serve,' he panted, turning into the dangerous tunnel. 'We serve our queen. We keep our colony.'

The tunnel was loud with flung earth and the snouting and clawing of the danger. Others were there, behind those doing the blocking. 'Let me by! Let me help save Her!' cried Dybbol. But cousins braced themselves there, several clotting the tunnel.

'Let me through! Make way!'

'We may not,' they said. 'Sniff yourself, man – smell how favoured you are now! Save yourself; we have plenty of warriors.'

'Myself? But we must save the queen!'

'We have plenty of brave. Run along and eat, and save up your strength.'

Dybbol turned back. His whole body swam with energy against the danger; his teeth ached to lock, his jaws to dig hard earth. He went to pantry and found a good rock-root, the biggest there and the hardest. He wrenched it out of the pile, and the pantry-wardens let him pass with it, making no murmur.

He gnawed and chawed all that day in a side-chamber. All the colony's doings came to him on the breezes past his nose, in tremblings and skitterings transmitted through the earth to his sensitive paws. No one called him, to watch, to work, to *anything*. He crouched, he ate, he slept – in daytime, slept! And in the night ventured to pantry again, past his fellows heaped in corners, their warmth cupped in the dormitory chambers and trailing down the breathy tunnels. And Dybbol gnawed, and slept, and gnawed, and listened to the colony all around him – its vast, safe busyness so wonderful – and slept . . .

. . . and awoke to the queen's screaming. 'Arraaaagh! Where is my-bold-one-my-Dybbol?'

He was fear all through, a throbbing thunder of it. The queen's voice caught him low in the spine and spread out from there. He sensed her turning in her chamber deep below, shoving her cousins away, shoving her cousin-cousins harder, roaring and shrieking. *The young are not in the queen-chamber*, the echoes told him. And not long afterward, *The cousins also are cleared. Her-Madam awaits you.* And the smell of the queen's greatest need, wild and sweet, spread through the colony. It crept into Dybbol's chamber and caught in the few outer hairs he had, around his nostril-folds, and clung there like thistle-fluff. He batted his own nose with his paws; he pressed his face into the earth wall, shaking all over.

Fighters came for him. He reared, he gaped, he hissed, frantic. There were too many of them.

'Come, now,' said Barraud. 'No one can escape the Queen's Notice.' And they dragged and shoved him, struggling, from the chamber. 'Good man,' said Barraud. 'Fight all the way. Make yourself delectable.' For the first time Dybbol's head-map of the colony failed him. He did not know where he was, only that the queen's need was strengthening towards him, winding its tingling tendrils into his spine, spinning terror out of his loins as mean and hot as snake-breath.

Then he was there, wrestled into the chamber by paramours and fighters. He tried to scrabble out, but they were digging, flinging earth, trapping him there with the roaring queen–

–who fell silent; who loomed up and clouted him to the floor with her great paw; who stood over him, lust-breath whistling in her mouth-hairs. And humming in his jaws, boiling along his body, moving his nerveless paws for him was that fierce, new, intensely sweet scent that twirled out of the queen, behind.

He dreamed he was young again, in a heap of young, interleaved with cousins. He chirped weakly, and they shifted, and their warmth intensified against him, pulsed him softly back to sleep.

He woke in pain, from nose-bristle to tail-nub – and alone, in a chamber too small for a dormitory. The only sounds were above him.

Amkarra came in, rolling a new-cut sweetbulb.

'Where am I, Amkarra?' said Dybbol. 'Where is this chamber?'

'Why, right by Barraud's, of course, along from our Deepest Heart.' She pushed the bulb towards him. 'This is for you.'

He found a feeble voice. 'Enjoy it with me, cousin.'

She put down her face. 'I may not, bold one, queen's paramour. But I hope it fills you as your children fill the queen, for our colony's prosperity.'

'For our colony's prosperity . . .' He lifted to the bulb a paw that shook with weakness.

Amkarra abased herself and backed away down the tunnel. Dybbol felt her go, her earthy fighter-smell fading under his own sweet reek. Then the fresh breath of the sweetbulb asserted itself, and he turned from the tunnel and began to gnaw.

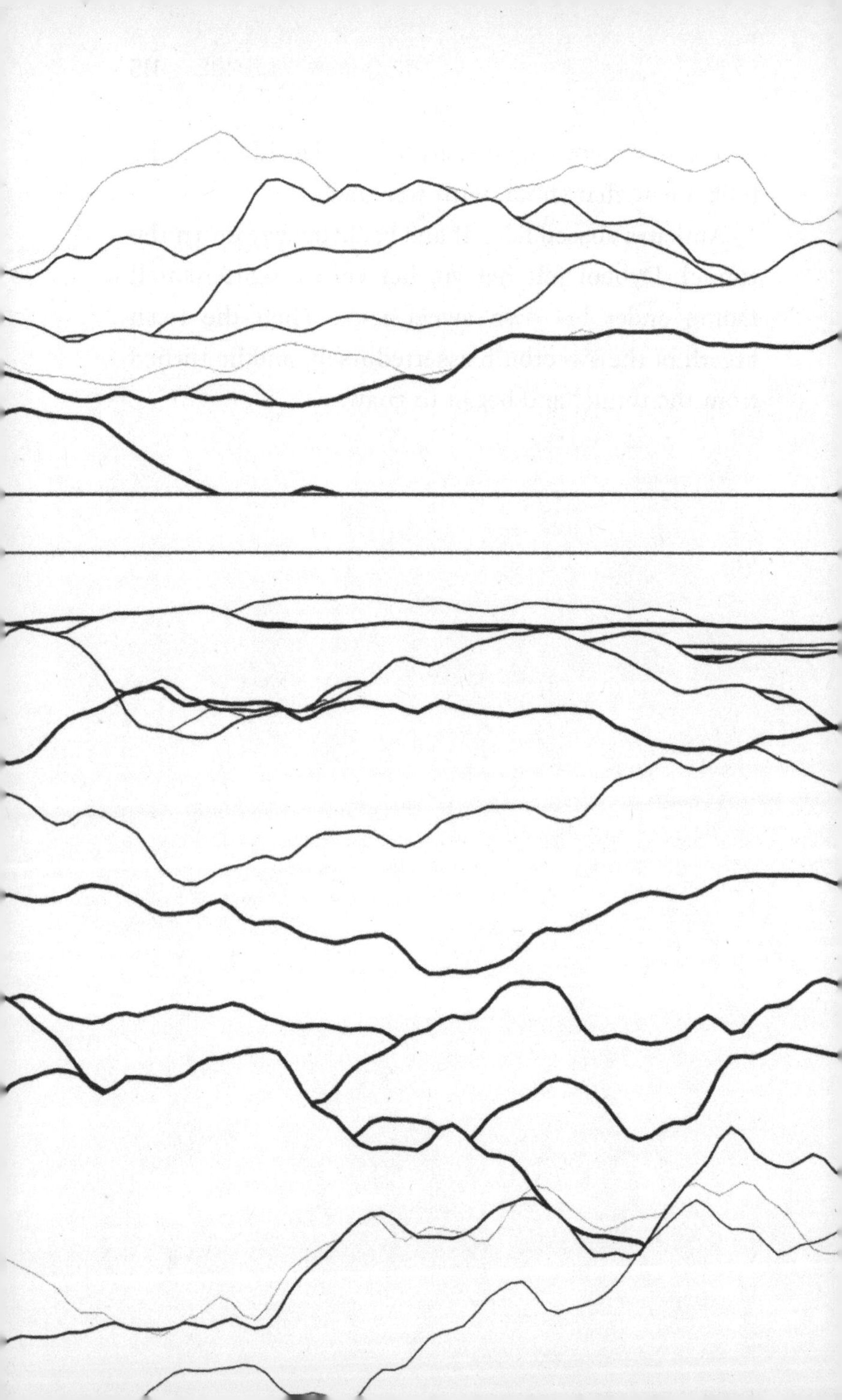

LEANNE HALL

Leanne is the author of two novels for young adults, the Text Prize-winning *This Is Shyness* and its sequel *Queen of the Night*. Leanne has had shorter pieces published in *Meanjin, The Age, The Best Australian Stories* and the anthology *Growing Up Asian In Australia*. Her work plays with the borders of reality and fantasy.

THE BREAKTHROUGH

'Minty,' says the clinic receptionist, 'Ms Mahfouz is running twenty minutes late.'

'No problem,' I say, even though I'm twitchy as anything. I settle down further into my seat and try not to tap my feet. I hope Melinda, Ms Mahfouz, won't be disappointed that my 'monumental personal revelation' didn't happen during one of our sessions. I mentally rehearse what I have to tell her.

It happened on Saturday night. I'm not in the habit of sneaking out for parties, and neither is my best friend, Queenie, but extreme circumstances drove us to it.

We waited until her mum had gone to bed and then we climbed out of Queenie's bedroom window.

The plan was to walk the train line all the way to Leila Morrow's house, a plan that I regretted in the first kilometre. Queenie walked on the tracks but I was on the pedestrian path that snaked along above. It turned out that even the path was dangerous – narrow and lumpy, with no lights. I was feeling creeped out, because Queenie had filled my head all week with ideas of demons and avenging monks. Oh, and a blister had formed on my little toe. No one takes blisters seriously, but they can go septic and result in amputation.

'Hoo hoo!' I called out, and then waited for Queenie's matching response. No answer.

'Queens?'

I leant over the railing in a panic, but Queenie was there on the tracks, her red hair flaring in the night.

'You didn't reply!'

'We wouldn't need a signal if you came down here.'

One day Queenie is going to dump me because I'm no fun, but there was *no way* that I was going to walk along the train tracks. My foot could have got stuck under a sleeper. A train could have mowed us down before we even knew what was happening.

'You know I've been psychologically scarred by my mum always going on about how I could be accidentally hurt or killed at any moment,' I told her. 'Melinda says that kind of conditioning is very hard to overcome. I haven't had a can of soft drink for years because I can't stop imagining that a European wasp might have flown inside the can.'

Queenie sighed deeply, confirming my theory that she's jealous that I have a therapist and she doesn't. 'We need to hurry, Minty.'

She was wearing short shorts that night, an oversized cardigan, a hybrid baseball-cap/beanie thing and platform boots. Her look was straight out of her favourite Tokyo street style Instagram.

Sometimes when I talk to Melinda about Queenie, I imagine that I'm reading Melinda's mind.

Melinda: *Minty has difficulty expressing her own wishes around such a forceful personality. JUST LIKE WITH HER MOTHER.*

'Remind me what our plan is?' I asked.

Actually that will be the wrong place to start. I'll need to rewind and explain to Melinda *why* we were gate-crashing an exclusive Year Twelve party – us, mere Year Tens with no taxi money and no plan!

A few weeks ago, Queenie and I were sitting near the basketball courts at lunch, both of us rushing. We'd snuck off campus to get Queenie a bubble cup so she had at least a kilo of sugar in her system from her mango grass jelly tea. Meanwhile, I had heart palpitations because we'd broken school rules.

Queenie was spying on Dominic Lopata and Nadia Drake – the king and queen of the school. They were pretending to practise lay-ups, but there was a lot of unnecessary body contact going on.

It was a confusing moment, because earlier this year, when I'd decided for sure that I was bisexual, I was a *major appreciator* of both Dom and Nadia (even though I was aware neither would consider a Year Ten). I hadn't known at the time that it was just a phase and after we watched that doco in health class, I realised (55–60% certain anyway) that I'm asexual. I wish I knew for sure though, because I'll have to make an announcement about it one day. I'd like to get the whole thing sorted before the end of high school.

'I do NOT like her,' said Queenie.

'Why? Everyone likes Nadia.'

Nadia has only been at our school since the start of the year, but there's school-wide consensus on this fact. She's pretty but not intimidating, smart but not too smart. She's also basketball obsessed, and plays on the usually bro-only school courts. These days there's half a court reserved for Nadia and her lady posse (one of which, I should note, is Leila Morrow). This is a significant advancement in gender relations at our school, and while I'm officially anti-sport, I still appreciate the progress.

Queenie sucked on her tea. 'Because she's pretending to be someone she's not.'

'Funny, that's exactly what everyone says about you.'

Queenie's scary blues focussed on me for a moment and then slid back to Dom and Nadia.

I reversed frantically. 'You know, because of the way you do your eyeliner? And your rabbit ears phonecase and the K-pop posters in your locker.' The more I tried to stem the flow of words, the more they spilt out. 'You like Pocky, you wear that floral backpack . . .' Everyone thinks it's hilarious that Minty Chan is besties with an Anglo who is more Asian than she is.

'Shhh! I've been watching Nadia zoom in on Dom for weeks. You know what she reminds me of? A snake – watch her.'

It's true that Nadia had a sinuous way about her. We watched her dribble the ball and then shoot. Her whole body rippled when she moved.

'Her eyes are too green to be real,' Queenie continued. 'She's probably wearing contact lenses to mask her elliptical pupils.'

'Elliptical pupils? What?'

But Queenie was already up and off the bench. The bell for the end of lunch rang as she crossed the court towards Dom. Nadia had slunk off with Leila Morrow.

'The movie, remember?' she called back to me. 'You know, that one with the sorcerer and the white snake?'

It took me a few seconds to recall the movie we'd seen months ago at Chinatown Cinema. Queenie had picked it because Jet Li was in it, only to be disappointed because he played a monk, and he's getting kind of old. I couldn't see the connection between the movie and Nadia though.

I hovered at a distance, while Queenie accosted the most popular boy at Glenwood High.

'You should stay away from Nadia,' she told Dom as he retied his shoes. 'She's hiding something. She's not who she says she is.'

Dom was extra-smirky. 'Let me guess, I should stay away from her . . . and go out with you?'

Queenie delivered a withering gaze.

'I'm well aware, Dominic Lopata, that I haven't fully physically developed yet, and definitely not enough for someone whose main hobby appears to be checking out the wide variety of fun bags at this school.'

That shut Dom up.

'Nadia wields a very ancient power. She'll go wild with love and then everything will be ruined. Heed my words!' Queenie was getting a bit melodramatic by this point. She's the best actress in Year Ten, after all.

'You're crazy,' muttered Dom, and caught up to his friends.

Queenie and I walked slowly to fifth period biology.

'Nice speech,' I said. 'Good use of the phrase *fun bags.*'

I already knew I was going to be dragged into something; I was used to Queenie's elaborate theories.

The wind picked up, throwing empty chip packets and leaves around the yard.

'I have to expose her,' Queenie said. 'I'm like the monk in the movie. My mission is to stop their forbidden love. I just have to figure out how.'

I tried to remember the storyline of the movie. It came back in bits and pieces. Susu, the White Snake demon, falls in love with an ordinary fisherman guy called Xu Xian. Susu is a good demon though, and disguises herself as a human so she can marry the clueless Xu Xian. But when Jet Li – the monk – figures this out, he's not happy. According to him, a human and demon can't be together and he spends the rest of the movie trying to break them up. They don't call White Snake and Xu Xian the Chinese Romeo and Juliet for nothing.

Now Queenie's comment about elliptical pupils made sense. In her delusional (maybe brilliant) brain, Nadia Drake was a love-mad snake demon.

The faint thump of music could be heard from the footpath. We pushed open the side gate of Leila's house and crept along the path. The noise and light increased.

At that stage I thought Queenie's theory was highly implausible, but I still couldn't completely rule it out. I was almost sick with worry about what might happen next though.

At the back of the house, we saw the Year Twelves milling under the carport and around the patio and pool. The boys and girls were mingling and no one was spewing, which would never happen at a Year Ten party.

We crouched behind the rock wall that circled the garden.

'Look!' Queenie whispered.

Dom and Nadia were twined together near the barbecue. Dom had his hands in Nadia's hair and was mashing his face against hers. Nadia grabbed Dom's butt and face-mashed back. I couldn't help wondering what it would be like to kiss with a forked reptilian tongue.

'What are we going to do?' It was hard to get my voice to come out. Meanwhile, Queenie looked calm as anything.

'I'm very glad you asked that, Minty.'

Queenie held out a tiny bottle, barely three

centimetres tall, made from green glass with a dragon moulded into its curves. It looked like something from my grandfather's bathroom cabinet, only more sinister.

'We're going to poison her?' I started hyperventilating, gulping noisily.

'Get a grip, Minty! Don't you remember the story? White Snake drinks the sulphur-flower wine and it causes her to reveal her true serpent form. Dom is going to be disgusted when he realises that he's been *licking a snake.*'

'But . . . how do we make her drink it?'

I was already imagining being arrested and charged for drink spiking. What would I look like in prison overalls? I tried to squish my head between my knees when I felt like I might faint.

'We have an ally. Leila's brother.'

Somehow Queenie managed to drag me back down the side of the house to a high-up window. She rapped on the glass three times, and then it slid up.

'There's a milk crate in the bush over there,' said a boy's voice.

We found the crate and stood on it. We were looking through the window into Sammy Morrow's bedroom.

'Hi,' I waved, trying to act normal. Sammy nodded back from his bed. We have French together.

'You got the stuff?' he asked. Queenie held up the bottle.

'The thing is, I'm feeling pretty comfortable at the moment,' Sammy said. 'This comic is great. And my chair is all the way over there.' His wheelchair was at the foot of his bed. 'It will probably cost you extra.'

'Like what?'

'Like . . . how about Minty's scarf?'

I loved that stripy scarf, but at that stage, losing it was the least of my worries. I unwound it and fed it through the window. Sammy took the scarf, and the tiny glass bottle.

'I'll see you in the back.'

We waited in the bushes for what seemed like eons before Sammy rolled towards the party, my purple and green scarf already around his shoulders.

'He'll never be able to pull it off,' I murmured.

Sammy cut in on Dom on the dance floor, wheeling in front of Nadia and jerking his chair back and forth. He waved his arms wildly and did some wheelies. Nadia seemed impressed.

Sammy beckoned her down to say something in her ear, and as she did, he poured the contents of the tiny green bottle into Nadia's beer. Moments later he glided away.

Queenie crowed with triumph. 'And now, we wait.'

She pulled her cardigan around her and sat on a rock nearby.

I settled against the fence, my eyes started drooping. It was probably all the adrenaline fleeing my body. 'How long will it take? I'm tired.'

Time stretched and folded as the Year Twelves cavorted under the starry sky. I had time to think.

The monk in the movie was kind of bigoted. He kept going on about how unnatural White Snake and Xu Xian's love was, and you didn't have to think that hard to realise it was like someone who thought people of different races or same sexes shouldn't be together. But then White Snake went so crazy when she almost lost Xu Xian, in a way that had made me think she was in love with the idea of love itself.

I tried to keep my eyes on Nadia but I reckoned the liquid in the miniature bottle had probably only been cordial. My energy was waning.

I woke up though, when someone threw Leila in the pool.

'The pool!' Queenie almost shouted. 'Why didn't I think of that? Those serpents practically lived in the water!'

Like lemmings jumping off a cliff, the Year Twelves hurtled into the freezing cold pool after her.

Some boys took off their shirts, others jumped in fully clothed. Girls shrieked as they hit the water.

Dom tried to talk Nadia into jumping, but she just swayed slightly. Eventually Dom gave up and did a massive running bomb.

'It's working . . .' said Queenie, as Nadia closed her eyes and collapsed into the pool.

There was an eerie silence, and then the screaming started.

Queenie and I jumped from our hiding place and reached the pool fence as everyone pulled themselves onto the pool deck like gasping fish. They stumbled away, tripping over with confusion and fear.

The water churned into froth. Dark shadows gathered deep down. I gripped the fence as the shadows coalesced and rose through the water. Something broke the surface and shot into the air: a scaly neck as thick as a tree trunk.

'It's true . . .' I whispered, to no one in particular.

The lady serpent drew herself up high above the gathering, showering the yard with water. Her rippling scales were peacock blue and green. Despite the snarling mouth and slitted eyes, I still recognised something of Nadia in the way she moved.

I looked to Queenie, but we had swapped positions; she was curled into a ball on the ground with her arms clasped around her head.

Blood tingled in my veins, but it was my turn to be strangely calm – I was the eye of the storm.

Nadia coiled and thrashed. She screeched, a haunting cry that echoed over the tidy roofs.

The Year Twelves were all huddled inside the house, looking out the windows with shocked faces.

The only person who wasn't afraid was me, Minty Chan.

I gazed skywards. Something odd had come over me. What a wonderful creature she was.

It occurred to me in that wondrous moment that I had a *thing* for snakes. Not a sexy-thing, necessarily, but a some-thing, a connection to Nadia. From the corner of my eye I saw Dom and a few of the others creep back into the pool area. Dom had picked up a deck chair, and his friends had armed themselves with bottles, barbecue tongs, whatever they could lay hands on.

I threw myself over the pool fence, and stood in between the boys and the pool.

'I will protect her at all costs!' I yelled.

Nadia dipped her head, fangs sharp like swords. She hissed, and Dom and his gang fell back.

Nadia's peculiar green eyes rolled. She nodded at me approvingly before heaving her body from the water. She slithered across the backyard, rolling over everything in her way like an armoured tank.

'You can go in now, Minty.'

The receptionist's voice breaks my reverie.

I stand and smooth my school dress. I feel nervous all of a sudden.

In the days since the party, I've waited for Nadia to return and give me instructions. Even though Queenie figured out who she was first, she's refused to talk about what happened, not even when some of the Year Twelves uploaded the videos they'd taken from the kitchen window.

The walls of the clinic are lime green and the corridor is lined with tasteful artwork. I reach Melinda's door.

If I can be servant, or admirer, or consort or whatever to a powerful lady-demon, then I can *definitely* stop worrying about what subjects to do next year, or what to study at uni. My anxiety about the future is totally gone.

Melinda is sitting in her armchair, and the couch and box of tissues are waiting for me. As always, her smile is warm and welcoming.

I can't wait to tell her.

COURTNEY BARNETT

Courtney is a Melbourne-based singer-songwriter and guitarist. Known for her witty, stream-of-consciousness lyrics and deadpan vocal style, she has enjoyed a rising profile since first coming to light in 2012 when she released an EP, *I've Got a Friend Called Emily Ferris*. In 2013, Courtney was invited to perform at New York's music showcase CMJ Music Marathon. Her first full-length album, *Sometimes I Sit and Think, and Sometimes I Just Sit*, was released in March 2015, for which she won three ARIA Awards.

AVANT GARDENER

I sleep in late
Another day
Oh what a wonder
Oh what a waste.
It's a Monday
It's so mundane
What exciting things
Will happen today?
The yard is full of hard rubbish it's a mess and
I guess the neighbours must think we run a meth lab
We should amend that
I pull the sheets back
It's 40 degrees
And I feel like I'm dying.

Life's getting hard in here
So I do some gardening
Anything to take my mind away
  from where it's sposed to be.
The nice lady next door talks of green beds
And all the nice things that she
  wants to plant in them
I wanna grow tomatoes on the front steps.
Sunflowers, bean sprouts, sweet corn and radishes.
I feel pro-active
I pull out weeds
All of a sudden
I'm having trouble breathing in.
My hands are shaky
My knees are weak
I can't seem to stand
On my own two feet
I'm breathing but I'm wheezing
Feel like I'm emphysem-in'
My throat feels like a funnel
Filled with weet bix and kerosene and
Oh no, next thing I know
They call up triple o
I'd rather die than owe the hospital
Till I get old
I get adrenalin
Straight to the heart

I feel like Uma Thurman
Post-overdosing kick start
Reminds me of the time
When I was really sick and I
Had too much psuedoefedryn and I
Couldn't sleep at night
Halfway down high street, Andy looks ambivalent
He's probably wondering what I'm
  doing getting in an ambulance
The paramedic thinks I'm clever cos I play guitar
I think she's clever cos she stops people dying
Anaphylactic and super hypocondriactic
Should've stayed in bed today
I much prefer the mundane.
I take a hit from
An asthma puffer
I do it wrong
I was never good at smoking bongs.
I'm not that good at breathing in.

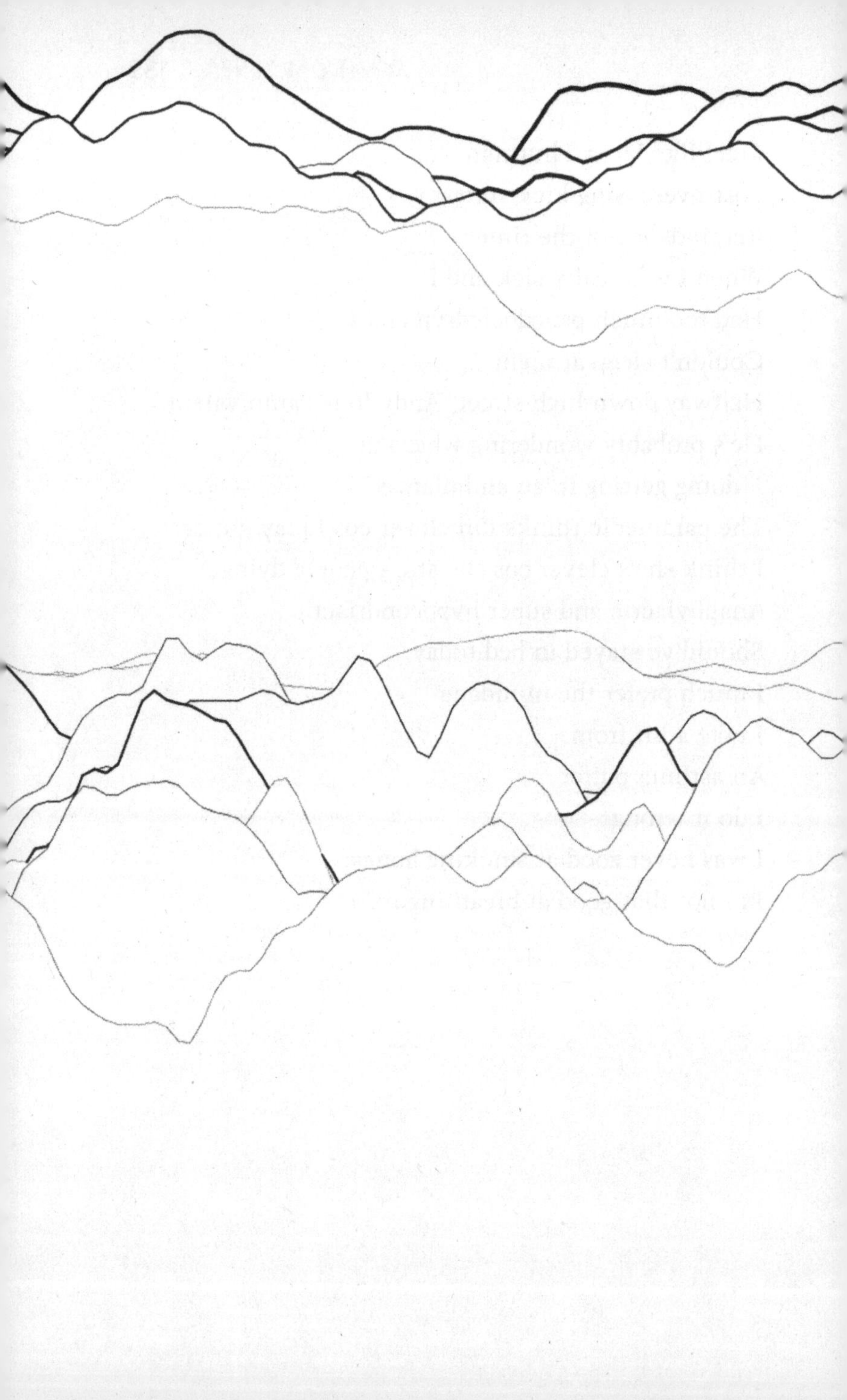

Shivaun is a children's and YA writer. Her debut novel about a girl called Frankie is titled *Frankie,* and her activity book about Medieval Europe is called *Medieval Europe*. She's inventive like that.

Her short fiction, flash fiction, essays and poetry have been published in *Above Water*, *Text*, *Vivid* and *The Victorian Writer*, and when she's not writing, she's beavering away as an editor and manuscript assessor. You can visit her at shivaunplozza.com or *@ShivaunPlozza*.

THE POINT

The caravan stinks of tinned pineapple. I breathe through my mouth and watch Claire's mum empty another tin into the glass bowl: a waterfall of golden chunks and piss-coloured juice.

'That's bullshit,' says Claire. She picks at the cut-offs riding up her bum and slumps into the bench seat beside me. I shuffle across to give her room.

'I just don't want you parading about the place dressed like a floozy.' Claire's mum jiggles the tin, shaking out the last few drops. 'And mind your language.'

'It's like a hundred degrees and we're at the beach. What the hell else am I going to wear?'

'I said mind your –'

'Hell's not a swearword, Mum. Fuck. Shit. Asshat. Dicksneeze. They're swear words.'

'Claire!'

I cover my mouth and pretend to cough.

'You see?' Claire's mum waves the butcher's knife at me. 'Susannah is so disgusted by your potty-mouth she's trying not to throw up.' She angles the cutting board over the bowl and scrapes in a mound of grated carrot.

Claire tugs down her bikini top. She hasn't got the boobs to stop it riding up. She says she'd kill to have my tits but she isn't the one whose school dress popped open when she was giving a presentation on volcanoes last year. They still call me Mount Ver-Suzie-Tits.

Even Claire.

Claire's mum adds a jug of orange jelly and stirs. She's making Sunset Surprise: pineapple, carrot, orange jelly, vomit. Only my dad is game to try it, but that's because a sheep kicked him in the head when he was ten and he lost his sense of taste.

She jabs at us again, this time with a wooden spoon. 'I was spitting chips when Carol told me she saw you hanging round those local boys. "Draped all over them and with her hoo-ha hanging out her shorts," she said.'

'Like I give a shit what that nosy bitch says.'

'Claire!'

Claire's Aunt Carol is an A-grade bitch but she's right about Claire: last night she nicked off round the back of the toilet block with Nick Paulson's cousin. Left me alone with Nick.

'Go and get changed,' says Claire's mum. 'There's that dress I got you for Christmas.'

Claire shoves two fingers down her throat and gags. 'Sure. And how about a pair of Carol's giant fuck-me-not undies?' She grabs my arm as she stands. 'Come on, Suz. We're going.'

Claire's mum shoots her a filthy look but says, 'Be a dear and open the fridge.' I know she's talking to me because she never asks Claire to be a dear. She slides the bowl off the bench and waits.

I open the fridge and edge out of her way but there's not much room in the caravan so I clip the side of the bowl and Sunset Surprise sloshes all over my arm.

'Oh poo,' says Claire's mum.

Claire snorts with laughter. I glare at her. 'Take a joke, Suz,' she says. 'That shit is funny.'

Claire's mum steadies the bowl; orange jelly rocks up and down the sides. 'Go and put that dress on, Claire. I'm not asking you twice.'

I look round for a tissue, a tea towel, anything; the jelly and pineapple juice tighten against my skin: sticky, tacky.

'Jeeze, Suz. Move your fat arse. I'm leaving without you.' Claire jumps from the top step and into the annexe.

I wipe my arm with the bottom of my tee and follow.

In the annexe, I step over Claire's brothers on their blow-up beds fighting over a PSP. Lucky Claire and me have our own tent this year.

'God, does my mum ever shut up?' Claire drags me out of the annexe and into the sun. It bites into the back of my neck. 'Hey, do you think we'll run into Nick at the surf club?'

I stop. Her arm stretches taught like a leash, still holding onto me. 'What?' she says.

'Aren't you going to change?'

'You're joking, right? I'm not wearing that boner-killing dress. But if you wanted to change . . .' she tilts her head, scanning my boxy tee and the boardies that used to belong to my brother '. . . I'll wait.'

When I stay silent, her look softens, eyes on my hips. 'I'm sure I've got something you could borrow.'

I shake my head. Her bellybutton ring winks at me, catching the light.

'Whatever,' she says, turning to leave. 'Don't say I didn't offer.'

Claire makes us hang outside the surf club for half an hour, but Nick and his cousin aren't there.

Good. I don't want to see Nick Paulson. I mean, I do, just, maybe in a different life.

In this life, the sea air makes my hair frizz. I could cover it with a hat, but the only one I own is pale blue denim with a plastic daisy on the front. I'm sure it looks cute on a five-year-old. I'm sure plenty of five-year-old boys would ask me to play doctors and nurses with them if I wore it, but Nick's nineteen and cute doesn't get you laid. That's what Claire says.

And stinking like pineapple can't help.

Claire shields her eyes, searching the foreshore. 'Let's try the beach.'

The bay is shaped like a horseshoe – that's good luck, right? I've been coming to Port Beacon with Claire's family forever, so long that I have memories of Nick with braces, zits and gangly, baby-horse limbs. He's tall now. Better hair. Straight teeth.

When we first started spending summers here, Claire and me used to dunk each other in the estuary behind the campground. We'd catch minnows with our bare hands and race each other to the top of the lookout. We used to throw rocks at Nick and his cousin from our fortress in the sand dunes.

Today we lie on the beach because Claire doesn't want to go in the water. Not yet. She stretches out on her towel and scans the beach. 'This place is so boring,' she says. 'There's no one even here.'

Kids run screaming past, arms and legs spazzing out as they race to the water. The beach is dotted with sun tents, eskies and sunbaked, red-raw skin.

'I know,' I say.

Claire and me share minimum chips at lunch, doused in vinegar and tomato sauce. She's full after four chips so I eat the rest. In the afternoon I convince her to swim to the pier. Halfway out we tread water and talk about Nick's cousin.

'He's a dickhead,' says Claire. 'I can't believe I got with him.'

I let my chin dip below the surface, salty water lapping in and out of my open mouth.

She told me everything already, last night in our tent. 'Too much tongue, not enough dick,' she said and I laughed into my pillow as she mimicked his grunts.

'Sorry I left you with Nick. God, what did you two even talk about?'

'Not much.'

Last night me and Nick sat on the picnic table opposite the toilet block. I stared at my toes, scrunching them up tight and then releasing them again. He'd talked about footy, uni, his dad, the car he wants to buy and how he got the scar on his arm.

'I like him,' I tell her.

Claire splashes me, her nose scrunched up. 'Serious? Nick Paulson?'

I nod.

That whole time on the picnic table, I'd waited. I'd waited for him to take my hand and lead me behind the toilet blocks too. But Claire and Nick's cousin had come back too soon.

'Nick's hot but . . . Do you think he likes you back?'

The sun stings my cheeks as I splash her. 'Yeah. Maybe.'

She laughs.

'What?'

She swims back to shore and I follow.

At least I can't smell pineapple any more.

We gather our stuff and leave the beach. My hair clumps in salty strands and my boardies cling to my thighs. Claire heads up the boat ramp, squeezing water from her hair.

'I am *not* playing cards while Mum gets drunk and Carol goes on about her fucking dog. Not again. There has to be something better happening in this town.'

Two lanky boys are leaning against the surf club wall, wearing bright-coloured boardies and grins. I'd recognise that tussle of gold-streaked hair anywhere.

'Hey,' says Claire, 'Is that –'

I grab her. 'Let's go back to the caravan. I want to get changed.'

'Don't be a killjoy.' She shakes me loose and waves at the boys. 'You're such a baby sometimes.'

'Hey,' says Nick, pushing off the wall as we near.

I look at his feet. Long toes. Covered in sand.

'Hey, yourself.' Claire runs her hand along the smooth, tanned skin of her belly. She doesn't look at Nick's cousin. 'What's happening?'

'Nothing.' Seawater drips from Nick's fringe. 'Been swimming?'

'Out to the pier and back.'

There's sand between my toes too.

'Cool,' says Nick.

Nick's cousin picks at the grout on the surf club wall. He's not as tall as Nick – skinnier, sharper features. But they look a little alike. The eyes, I think. The corner of the mouth. He nudges Nick's shoulder. 'Are we going? I'm bored.' He glances at Claire. She doesn't look back.

'We're headed to The Point,' says Nick. There's a trail of fine, golden hair leading from his belly button to the waistband of his shorts. He nudges my arm and when I look up he's smiling at me, eyes scrunched up against the sun. 'Coming, Suz? Wouldn't be a party without you.'

My throat tightens. 'I –'

Claire grabs his arm. 'Let's go,' she says. 'I'm game.'

The Point is where you go to get high, make out or kill yourself. Years ago some guy tied up his wife and kids in the back of his Commodore and pushed it over the cliff edge. The car got stuck on the rocks below but it didn't matter; he'd already shot them.

We duck under the Norfolk pines and jump the railing. Nick's cousin stands behind a group of old people, pretending to wank himself.

Claire grabs my arm, pulling me close. 'He's such a loser,' she says, her breath damp against my ear. 'I don't care what he says. I'm not getting with him again.'

It's a steep walk, beside the road at first but then we verge right, heading out onto the bluff, nothing but low scrub and sand-coloured rocks.

'Did you see the fucker's teeth?' says Nick's cousin. He won't shut up about a shark his dad caught this morning. 'Imagine it giving you a blowie.'

'Gross,' says Claire.

'Nah, you should have seen it. Dad pulled it onto the pier and there was blood everywhere. That's when I knew it was a girl shark.'

'Rank,' says Claire.

'What do you reckon?' Nick's cousin nudges me. 'Was it on the rag or just had its cherry popped?'

I bite the inside of my lip and look away.

'Don't talk about being a virgin in front of Suz,' says Claire.

'Why?'

I'm sunburnt; my skin stings with the heat.

'You know,' says Claire. She covers a smile with her hand.

Nick's cousin grabs my arm: sweaty fingers. 'Wait. You're not . . .? Shit, that's sad.'

I shake free and hurry up the path. He laughs.

'Lay off her,' says Nick.

'No seriously. I can sort that out for you, Suz.'

Claire snorts. 'Yeah. It'll only take three seconds.'

Nick's cousin gives her a filthy look.

'Come on, dickhead,' says Nick, pushing his cousin square in the back.

He smiles at me, leans in and whispers, 'Besides, two seconds is his limit.'

I grin.

The path grows wider, the scrub clears and then there's nothing but blue sky, blue sea. Nick grabs Claire around the waist, making like he's going to throw her over the edge.

She screams, 'Don't!' but she's laughing.

Last year the council built a wooden platform jutting out from the edge. I walk out and lean against the railing.

Nick cups his hands around his mouth. 'Don't jump!'

'Jump!' shouts his cousin.

Claire leans beside me, bumping shoulders. 'You're not angry, are you? I was just joking.'

When am I ever angry? I wasn't angry when she convinced me to wear her tight blue dress but laughed loudest of all when James Hadley called me a beached whale. I wasn't angry when she ditched me to start hanging out with Bianca Freeman and her coven of clones. I let her come crawling back when she'd screwed Bianca's boyfriend in the back of his dad's butcher van and the coven had started a hate campaign. I couldn't afford to be angry; I didn't want to be alone.

'It wasn't funny,' I tell her.

She turns, arms linked through the railings, arching her back. 'Yeah? Well if you knew how to take a joke, Nick might like you.'

The three of them share a joint, sitting in a circle in a clearing. Claire laughs heaps then rests her head in Nick's lap, fingers playing an imaginary piano. Nick offers me the joint but I shake my head.

The sun disappears.

'It's cold,' says Claire. Nick rubs her shoulder until she falls asleep.

'Need to take a piss,' says his cousin.

'Don't get your dick bitten off by a shark,' says Nick.

His cousin looks at Claire with her head in Nick's

lap. 'No sharks where I'm going.' He disappears into the scrub.

Nick stretches back, tilting his head to the sky. 'What do you reckon, Suz?'

I watch him, Adam's apple bobbing up and down like a fishing float.

'About what?'

He laughs. 'Life and shit.'

I brush sand from my feet and between my toes. 'It's okay.'

'Okay? It's fucking beautiful! Have you seen the stars? Look up, Suzie Q.'

I lift my chin and yeah, the stars are out and they're beautiful. I look at Nick.

'You see it, right?' he says.

I lick my lips and taste salt.

Last night he told me he never wanted to leave this town: 'Can't see stars in the city. And don't get pretty girls coming by every summer.'

He looks at me across the clearing and for once I don't look away.

'Can I ask you something?' he says.

I nod.

'Do you think . . .' He laughs. 'Shit. I'm usually better at this sort of thing.'

I lean forwards. And wait.

'I want to know . . .' He shifts forwards too, careful

to keep Claire from spilling out of his lap, but his eyes are solely on mine. My fingers twitch. 'I mean. Do you reckon . . . Do you think she likes me?'

My mouth is dry. 'She?'

'Claire.' He looks down, Claire's hair spilling like a golden waterfall down his shins. 'You and me are mates so I figured I could talk to you. Can you ask her for me?'

Nick's cousin stumbles back into the clearing. 'No sharks but a fucking bush tried to take me out.' He looks at his elbow, a dribble of blood pooling there. 'See that?'

Nick's looking at me, but only because he's waiting for an answer.

And I know what it's like to wait.

I lower my head, picking at the sand between my toes again. 'Yeah,' I say, a tremor in my voice that I can't hide. 'I'll ask.'

I sit on an esky outside the tent. It's dark and my eyes are stinging from all the sunscreen and salt water. Claire's mum isn't back yet; the twins are asleep in the annexe.

I watch the tent. The zip is closed. Rustling, giggling and grunting coming from inside. I just want to go to sleep.

I told Claire about Nick as we walked back to the

campground, the two boys lagging behind us. 'Sorry,' she said. 'But you're not surprised, right? I'm just more his type.'

I told her I didn't mind. I said I wasn't angry.

I squeeze my hand into a fist, nails digging into my palm until I'm sure I've left a mark. I should have gone with Nick's cousin; he left for the pub ages ago. Instead, I shiver and think about blue dresses, butcher vans, sharks and Nick Paulson.

I'm not angry.

But I am alone.

Feet crunch on the gravel, footsteps heading towards me. I look up.

'Susannah, love?' Claire's mum stumbles. Drunk. She's hugging the untouched bowl of Sunset Surprise. I move to her, prying the bowl free before she drops it. 'How come you're still up? Where's Claire?'

I look at the tent: silent, motionless. No way out except the flaps at the front. All I can smell is pineapple.

She places a hand on my forearm. 'Susannah?'

I think about blue dresses, butcher vans, sharks and Nick Paulson.

I look at Claire's mum. She's waiting. So I point. 'In the tent,' I say. 'With Nick Paulson.'

The tent swishes madly. 'Fuck's sake, Suzie,' shouts Claire from inside. 'Are you thick?'

Claire's mum grips tighter. She looks at the tent. 'Claire? You're not –?'

Claire yanks down the zip and stumbles out, tying her bikini. Nick's inside the tent, struggling into his boardies, flashing his bare arse.

'Claire! How could you?'

Laughter bubbles inside my throat. I cover my mouth, holding it in.

Claire's face is ugly with rage. 'You did that 'cause you're jealous.' She jabs my chest, right in the middle of Mount Ver-Suzie-Tits. 'Fat, ugly and jealous.'

Her mum gasps.

But I'm not angry.

'No, Claire,' I say and upend Sunset Surprise over her head. She screams. Chunks of pineapple slip into her open mouth; jelly and grated carrot cling to her chest. I set my laughter free – loud, unbridled. 'You just can't take a joke.'

WIL WAGNER AND LIZZIE WAGNER

Wil is a young singer-songwriter and the lead singer of Melbourne folk/punk/rock group The Smith Street Band. He began writing and performing as a teenager, and is known for his honest, personal and raw song-writing style. *Laika* is Wil's take on the fabled story of the dog sent on a Soviet mission into space in 1957.

Lizzie is a multi-disciplinary artist and designer who has recently graduated from RMIT where she studied Interior Design. Lizzie's interest in illustration and picture books prompted her to create a small, handmade book containing the lyrics from her brother Wil's song *Laika*. These illustrations were some of those featured in the book.

LAIKA

From here in my cage I see them make plans,
Hear them reassure investors, shake
presidents' hands.
The men with machines put tubes into me,
They measure my vital signs, my flight trajectory.
They taught me to sit, taught me to lie down.
Told me that a thousand years of
wondering would end now.
They fed me my last meal, was the same as my first.
From here in my cage, I watch the men work.

And now it's a flurry of lab coats and hurry.
They talk about budgets and taxpayers' money.
And I wag my tail and I be a good girl,
They forgot to walk me this morning they
were too busy changing the world.
And I'm out from my cage and I'm trying to be brave,
But the men they are sweating and
now they're injecting,
And as I awake
I'm shocked and amazed.
At the sheer, crushing empty.

And I look down on men's little earth, sitting
there quietly, wondering what it's worth.
And I drift away, but that's okay, there's more
room to play out here than back in my cage.

and i don't understand
because i'm not as smart
as them

And I know I will die, but that is fine,
Cause in some way I am helping mankind.
And I don't understand, cause I'm
not as smart as them,
But even a parachute would have
shown that they cared.

And so I float on, space's only dog.
Friend to the stars, pet of the sun.
From my little ship I dream of my bone,
A walk in the park, something comfy to sleep on.

And they call me Laika but I'd just like to say
That I was born Little Curly and
I'll die with that name.

PM FREESTONE

PM writes YA fiction, has published a handful of short stories, and is now working on novel-length projects. She is a graduate of the Clarion Writers' Workshop, a qualified archaeologist and a doctor of something philosophical. Her formative years were spent in drought-stricken rural Victoria. These days, she lives in rain-soaked Edinburgh, Scotland, where she speculates about random stuff – like how a Henry Lawson poem would read if it were set in the future.

You can find her on Goodreads, Twitter or at pmfreestone.com.

WHAT MATTERS IT NOW IF THE SOIL BE SOAKED?

I didn't grow up in this city.

Mum and I left the farm when I was fifteen. By then, the town and fields were made of dust. Everything had bled out and baked until it was powdered in dull red – bull-nosed iron verandahs, windmills toppled over bores long poisoned, power poles flanking roads as paper-thin as the shed skin of a lace monitor, the lines crisscrossing the backs of your hands. Dad said that if you've worked the land for generations, there's nowhere else for your heart. I lashed out like a stockwhip. I will always wish I could call back those words, but I'd flicked my wrist and the strike was inevitable: *Open your eyes. We have to leave. Or do you want us to die here, too?*

He lasted longer than the eucalyptus skeletons along the eroded Murray bed – root systems rather than branches reaching for the sky – but not by much. On the day Artesia's inspectors discovered his hacked filter rig, they issued a bill for the 'stolen' water and a hardware interference fine that would bankrupt the farm twice over. The day after, I found him in the old shearing shed. I lowered him to the carpet of desiccated sheep dung, pulled up the flannel collar of his shirt to hide the bruising, and folded his hands over his stomach. He looked peaceful, like he'd fallen asleep daydreaming in the golden wheat fields of bedtime stories. That's how I remember him. Even if nobody else can.

With the ashes scattered to the wind, I put as many pieces of Mum back together as I could find, and we left for the city.

I used to dream of going to uni, but the country state schools had dropped like flies before I was born, and there was no way my parents could have afforded private city fees. I'd kept up with the online modules the government still provided, though, so when Mum and I arrived down south, I sat sponsorship exams and scored offers from both HydrateVic and

Artesia. Everything in me wanted to go public. As a Government department HydrateVic at least *pretends* to care a drop about its people. But their terms were a joke. So, I gritted my teeth and took my only chance on a ticket out of here for me and Mum.

My contract with Artesia provides full fee coverage for the best private school in the city *and* a reserved place in a top Asian uni if I 'perform to expectations'. I guess big offers are small things from a company that owns the continent's largest aquifer, the de-sal, and every reverse osmosis filter from Melbourne to Mumbai. They already owned our lives, what was one more piece of paper?

The McKillop Hall welcome pack arrived a day later. Efficient. Every item, from school tie to stats textbook, was etched or printed or embroidered with Artesia's stylised fountain-of-life logo. There was a digitally signed motivational letter from the principal, noting they had 'taken the liberty' of including prospectuses to the 'most suitable' universities for McKillop graduates. Mum flicked through the colour-saturated photos that appeared on my shiny new tablet – an Edenic Laotian campus of palms and orchids half a world away. She hugged me, mustering a smile that hadn't softened her features in months. 'If you can't beat 'em, join 'em,' she said.

Dad *hates* that saying.

Hated, I mean. He scorned the 'big smoke', too. If he were walking beside me now, he'd be gibing at the fact that my feet carry me home from the first day of school faster than the sleek black sedans stuttering along the congested street. He'd tell me I'm twice as smart as their passengers because I earned my place, even though we all wear McKillop Hall's pleat skirt, blouse and blazer. I'd nod and wouldn't admit to wishing I was reclining on soft leather inside a cocoon of metal and tinted glass.

But Dad's not here. Instead, more guards than usual are stationed at the Irrigation Zone checkpoints. Before the buyout was in full swing, the IZ was a jigsaw of urban villages – individual characters with graffiti personalities and old-school Anglo names like Carlton, Richmond, Ascot Vale. Now the only thing that matters is whether a place has irrigation. Or not.

I hitch my schoolbag on my shoulder. Beyond the checkpoints, flames glow against the dusty twilight. Smoke mixes with exhaust fumes and my guts knot. It isn't my neighbourhood on fire. It's way further out. But still, shouts leap in the distance, reverberating with the sing-song rhythm of a schoolyard chant (though no skipping rope ditty I ever heard was punctuated with shattering windows). I guess Artesia's shut down another community hydrant – *purity is priceless*.

Up ahead, a girl in fatigues sprints towards the checkpoint. She sticks out like a bloody thumb among the suits and sponsored school uniforms. Long, dark hair whips across her face each time she checks over her shoulder. Sure enough, a pair of corp-cops rounds the corner too, semiautomatics slung over their backs as they pump their arms in pursuit.

As I hurry on, the girl detours from the main thoroughfare. Lithe and sure as the city's ubiquitous tabbies, she hurdles hedges, scales the rusting iron fence of a nearby apartment building and disappears over a low roof. When she drops to the pavement beside me, I startle and trip. The next thing I know, we're going down in a tumble of blue blazer, camo and fuck-off motorcycle boots.

'Watch it, water baby.' The venom in her voice punctures the air between us.

Breath exits my lungs as if I've had a fist to the stomach. But it's not because of her words, it's her eyes. They're huge, dark and brimming with, well, *injustice*. And they're staring at me.

'Uh, sorry.' I manage to stand and hold out a hand.

She ignores it and scrambles upright. 'Fucking typical.' A glance behind and she's off, boots thumping along the pavement, corp-cops in pursuit.

I watch her go and rub a bruised knee, now exposed through torn school tights. Great. That's the last thing I need on my first monthly sponsor report.

At the checkpoint, I press my ID to the scanner, trying to look like I belong. The Artesia logo glitters in the floodlights and the scanner flashes green. One of the soldiers claps a hand onto my shoulder. 'Don't take it personal, kid. She's feral.'

I perform the wry smile he expects and head for home.

The next afternoon, I sit on the bluestone wall beneath the welcome sign of McKillop Hall – *Where girls realise their worth* – watching the last of my classmates being chauffeured away. Who knows why I do this. I'd be less incongruous if I tattooed *weird new girl* across my forehead.

'You wish you were one of them, don't you?' A figure slinks from the shadow of the gates. She looks so different dressed in grey and royal blue, Artesia's crest emblazoned over her heart. But there's no mistaking those eyes.

Discovering we share a sponsor gives me an unfamiliar surge of confidence. I clear my throat and stick out my hand. 'Luce.'

'I know who you are, water baby.'

'I'm *not* one of them.'

'But you wish you were.' She points to the last of the dark cars disappearing around the corner. 'And that makes you worse than them, wouldn't you say?'

Heat prickles my cheeks.

'Sorry, I just get a bit sensitive about these things.' She rakes her fingers through her hair. In the sun, it's not just dark, it's as black and shiny as wet charcoal. This time she offers to shake. 'Mia.'

I take her hand and a chance on directness: 'What were you doing yesterday?'

She glances around, presumably making sure nobody's in earshot. 'What do you bloody well think? Protesting the buyout. Every section of the grid the Government flogs to Artesia means another price hike. No safety net for missed or late payments. *Nada*.'

I gesture to the crest on her blazer. 'But aren't you scared of losing your sponsorship? Of ending up out there for good?'

She laughs. The sound holds less joy than Artesia lets the de-sal spout water. 'Have you even *been* out of the IZ? Stepped foot in the Fringe? Walked with the ex-sponsored bums of Gerry Town?'

I glance away. I'd rather let her win than dredge up ghosts.

'Ah, Lucia. The blind saint, no?' Mia steps close, takes my hand in a beyond-greeting way and smiles with teeth so straight and white that I wonder if she scored a better health plan than me. Her palm warms my own and her breath flutters against my cheek.

'If more people don't take a stand, you'll do all that, and more. That'll be your life.'

Mia finds me when I'm hunched over in the girl's bathrooms stuffing wads of toilet paper in my armpits so that I don't sweat on my blazer. Unlike most of my classmates, I can't afford to launder my uniform fresh every week.

Over the last two years at McKillop, I've learnt that Mia terrifies half our year level and dominates the spank bank of most of the others (I still like to think myself an outlier, but I'm probably equal parts column A and column B). As she stands on the toilet in the next cubicle and peers over the partition, she has the grace to ignore my hand under my arm and the red splotches of embarrassment that creep from my unbuttoned shirt and mottle up my neck. But that's where politeness ends.

'What the hell are you dawdling in here for? It's at least an hour to get across the IZ. We're not going to make the protest if you don't get your arse in gear.' She somehow manages to pronounce the Irrigation Zone acronym 'easy' without a hint of irony.

Her kohl-rimmed eyes appear huge in a pale face unblemished by dirt or sun. If I wasn't already feeling like a rabbit with myxo, trembling and slow-witted, failing vision clouding friend from foe, her penetrating stare seals the deal.

'I'm not going.' I muster a drop of dignity and close my shirt. I hope she didn't get a glimpse of my bra. I've seen Mia change in gym class enough times to know she favours white lace. Mine has forgotten the colour it used to be.

'Are you for real? They're trying to apply this new filter fee *retrospectively*. Half the city will go dry if that gets through.'

'Keep your voice down,' I hiss.

'But *your house* is in that block.'

Only city-born would call it a house. It used to be a pub – a gathering place for drink and laughter. Now alcohol is the domain of the rich (who else can afford compensating for a diuretic?). So places like that have turned into living spaces for the rest of us to cram into. Mum and I took a room there when we came down south, with peeling paint and a fan that hangs precariously from the ceiling. I keep nagging her to let me take it down before it crashes to the floor between our twin beds, or worse, clocks one of us good in the middle of the night. But Mum's a believer. She still thinks the government will restore electricity to the building, as if reality isn't already written on the wall surer than the paint is unfurling from it.

Thinking of that hellhole stokes my anger, but I damp it down to nonchalance. 'So I'll scrounge a rain tank and jemmy a reverse osmosis filter. Your point?'

'Seriously, do you even remember when it last rained?'

'August fourth.'

She rolls her eyes. 'You've got to get active. Stand up for your rights.' She jumps down from her pedestal and speaks the next line from outside my cubicle. 'Or make your voice count for those who don't have one any more.'

I adjust the sleeves of my blazer, testing the paper under my arms. It holds. When I jerk the door open, the surprise sends Mia onto her back foot.

'How many times do we have to go over this? I've almost got the points I need for Laos. One more exam before graduation. *Not* the time to do anything . . . controversial.' I look pointedly at her on the last word – we both know it's a synonym for stupid.

Mia sniffs. 'Some of us don't have that kind of report card. And with a family like mine, I'm never leaving this city.' She turns away before I can study her expression. It's rare for either of us to ever mention the 'f' word. I keep my reasons snug against my chest, so I never question hers.

Crossing to the bench, Mia reaches inside her backpack. Her hand reappears holding a huge, rose-cheeked mango. I arch my brows so high my ponytail shifts on my scalp. Heady perfume wafts towards me.

'Where'd you get that?' My mouth waters around the accusation, though I'm pretty sure I'm salivating over stolen goods.

'Go halvies with me?'

'What's the catch?'

'Come to the march.'

I snatch up my bag in an attempt at haughty reproach, but the safety pin holding the zip together fails, sending my tablet clattering onto the tiles. The screen flashes to a book cover – black letters hemmed with bands of orange: Steinbeck. We're studying *The Grapes of Wrath* this year, like every year before us. It feels like someone's tongue-in-cheek joke.

I'll be damned if I'm anyone's punchline. I gather my things and leave Mia standing in the bathroom, speechless, for once.

Our room in the pub is one of the smallest, but it's near the fire escape so I chose it for Mum's sake. The external door is getting stiffer by the day, and this evening it takes my full weight to shoulder it open. I climb out onto the rickety stairs, over the bannister and onto the roof. To the south, skyscrapers form gleaming bridges between an audacious canopy of London plane trees and the brass sunset. The amount of water it takes to polish their mirror shine after every dust storm could supply my neighbourhood for years. No matter. Not that long from now I'll be assigned my engineering post in the Laotian hills. Mum and I will have rain on our faces and moss beneath our feet.

It's Thursday. Which means the water filter has been running. We've been hanging on just inside the IZ, but that doesn't mean the community can pay on-demand premiums. Sure, if Artesia rings the city's supply in further, we won't even have the tap that has provided this much. But Tiny Liza, the mountain of a woman who runs the house, has contacts inside HydrateVic. It'll be parched, but we'll survive on government credits.

My neighbours know about the little garden I keep up here, a row of potted succulents and cacti I've collected over the past two years, so they leave me their greywater. This evening their generosity – a four-inch pool in the bottom of the bucket left by the door – makes tears spring into my eyes. I blink them back. I've got my flaws, but I'm not indulgent.

I'm carefully rationing my bounty between aloe and miniature jade when voices ricochet from the street. I lean over the guttering to see a patrol car, stamped with the Artesia water fountain, and three corp-cops closing in on Tiny Liza. The landlady stands between the men and our filter hydrant, arms crossed over her broad chest.

'I told you, we already made the payment.'

One of the cops makes a show of checking his tablet. 'Not according to our records.'

Tiny Liza plants her hands on her hips. 'Then your records are wrong.'

A smile quirks my lips. She won't budge.

The cop with the tablet nods to the other two, and they loosen batons in their holsters.

'You can think again if you reckon I'm going to let you shut us off without a warrant.'

He brandishes the metal truncheon. '*This* is my warrant.'

Tiny Liza answers him with a right hook. He stumbles backwards, clutching his jaw, but his squad mate jumps into the gap, and the third circles the woman, slamming a metal bat across the back of her knees. She crumples forwards onto the cracked bitumen like a sack of imported grain. The second cop flips open the hydrant casing and removes the filter membrane, carrying it to the back of the squad car.

When the vehicle has disappeared from sight, I plunge down the fire escape. Tiny Liza has found her feet, though she leans heavily against the fence, pinching her nostrils and tilting her head back. I reach out to touch her arm, though stop short. 'Are you all right?'

'Never better, chookie,' she says, dry as February.

I cross to the filter. 'I can fix this, you know. There's expired membranes in the basement at school. They'll filter fine if I hack their meter chips. My da –' I pull myself up just shy of a memory flood. 'If I swap it back to the dodgy membrane before next inspection, those jerks will be none the wiser.'

'No, chookie. They'll find out eventually. We'll think up another way round it.' Tiny Liza's words are resilient but her eyes reflect defeat. She heaves herself up and lurches into the old beer garden.

I slump against the fence in her place, the corrugated iron still warm as dusk bruises to night. I want to protest to Tiny Liza's retreating back. Want to tell her I'll help my neighbours and damn the consequences. But my voice withers in my throat.

Typical, Mia's recrimination whispers through my thoughts.

I never thought I'd be here.

We're all individuals but we move with a hive mind, pressing forward, shouting slogans, each word somehow more than just sound and air pushing from our chests.

Mia's so close behind me that her breasts press against my back, her lips touch my ear. 'The screaming is the best part, don't you think? So liberating.' Her words send a shiver rippling through me.

She stoops and takes a cloth-wrapped package from her bag. 'Stay here.'

'What are you –?'

'We need to make this count.' She leans in and kisses me full on the lips, then pulls back, grinning the grin of the mad. I'm left holding her empty satchel as she disappears into the mob.

I shoulder both bags and survey the scene, trying to determine my next move. Moments after I find some space to stand, Mia reappears, running at full speed down the street. When she levels with me she grabs my hand. 'Run!'

There's a crack behind us like summer thunder. An unseen force slams into my back and it's all I can do not to fall face first onto the road. Pebbles and mortar and metal shower down on us. Only when the debris settles do I dare look behind, just as a river of muddy water flows over my feet, swirling around my ankles and channelling down the disused tram tracks. It stinks of sulphur, but it's quickly overpowered by the scent of burning. The corp-cops' focus returns to the front line, battling political and literal fire. Smoke billows around us. Have the houses caught?

The haze stings my eyes and suddenly I'm not surrounded by shouts and stamping feet.

I'm in a shearing shed.

A shearing shed I burnt down.

Because I couldn't bear the truth.

I lurch forward, desperately seeking the edge of the crowd.

'Luce,' Mia's voice sounds a long way off. 'Luce!'

I'm so stunned I don't notice the corp-cop until he has looped an arm around Mia's waist, yanking her hand from mine, dragging her backwards.

'Luce!'

I splash after her, pushing aside protestors and weaving wide of corp-cops. Mia kicks and scratches at her captor. He curses but doesn't show any signs of letting go.

I cast around me. The mouth of a laneway beckons, several of its bluestone cobbles loose. A few steps and a blink and I'm hefting a chunk of rock the size of a house brick. The soldier carries Mia from the fray and I follow, cobblestone tight in my hand. It's only when I slam the rock against the back of the soldier's neck, at the point where his helmet ends and before his Kevlar begins, that I realise the savage scream in my ears started in my own throat.

The corp-cop collapses, sending Mia sprawling to the ground. I offer her my hand, like I did the day we met. She lets me help her to her feet. The soldier lies still, one arm pinned beneath him. A thin line of blood trickles from his ear.

I vomit.

Then they're on us. Hands grab me from behind. Blue lights flash. My arms are yanked back. Steel cuffs snap over my wrists, almost wrenching my shoulders from their sockets like wings being torn from a roast chicken.

Mia's quicker than I am, she always has been. She ducks out of the way and melts into the crowd. As the corp-cops pile me into the back of a white van along with half a dozen other protestors, I desperately hope she's okay. But I can't do anything except wait, trussed and prone, eyes and throat burning with smoke and acid.

On the drive to Central District police station, we stop at a crossroad. A black limo pulls up next to us, stylised fountains glimmering from the executive-issue wheel hubs. Before the tinted window closes I catch a glimpse of the passenger lounging in the back seat, black hair spilling over her shoulder like a waterfall at night.

Recognition knifes through me: dark eyes in a pale face.

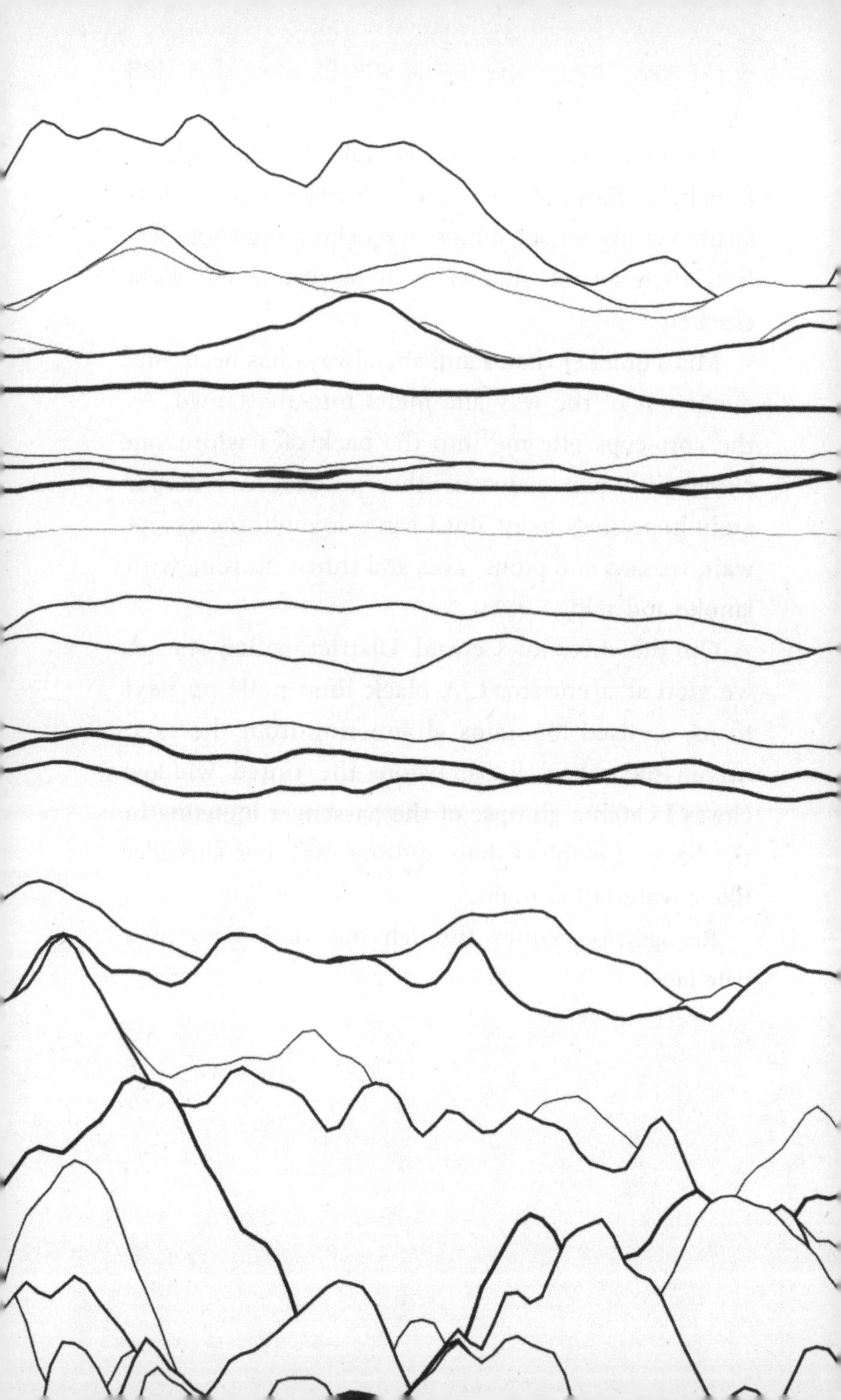

MEG CADDY

Meg has a Bachelor of Arts with Honours in Literature-cognate-History from the University of Western Australia. In 2013, her debut YA fantasy novel *Waer* was shortlisted for the Text Prize, which led to a book contract. Meg was the 2013 Young Writer-in-Residence at the Katharine Susannah Prichard Writers' Centre, and has been working with children of all ages for the last six years. She loves storytelling, pirates and her pet lizard Hotshot.

Meg would like to acknowledge and thank Gemma Goepel, Kristin Lane and Beverly Twomey for sharing their expertise in *The Lord of the Rings* replica swords.

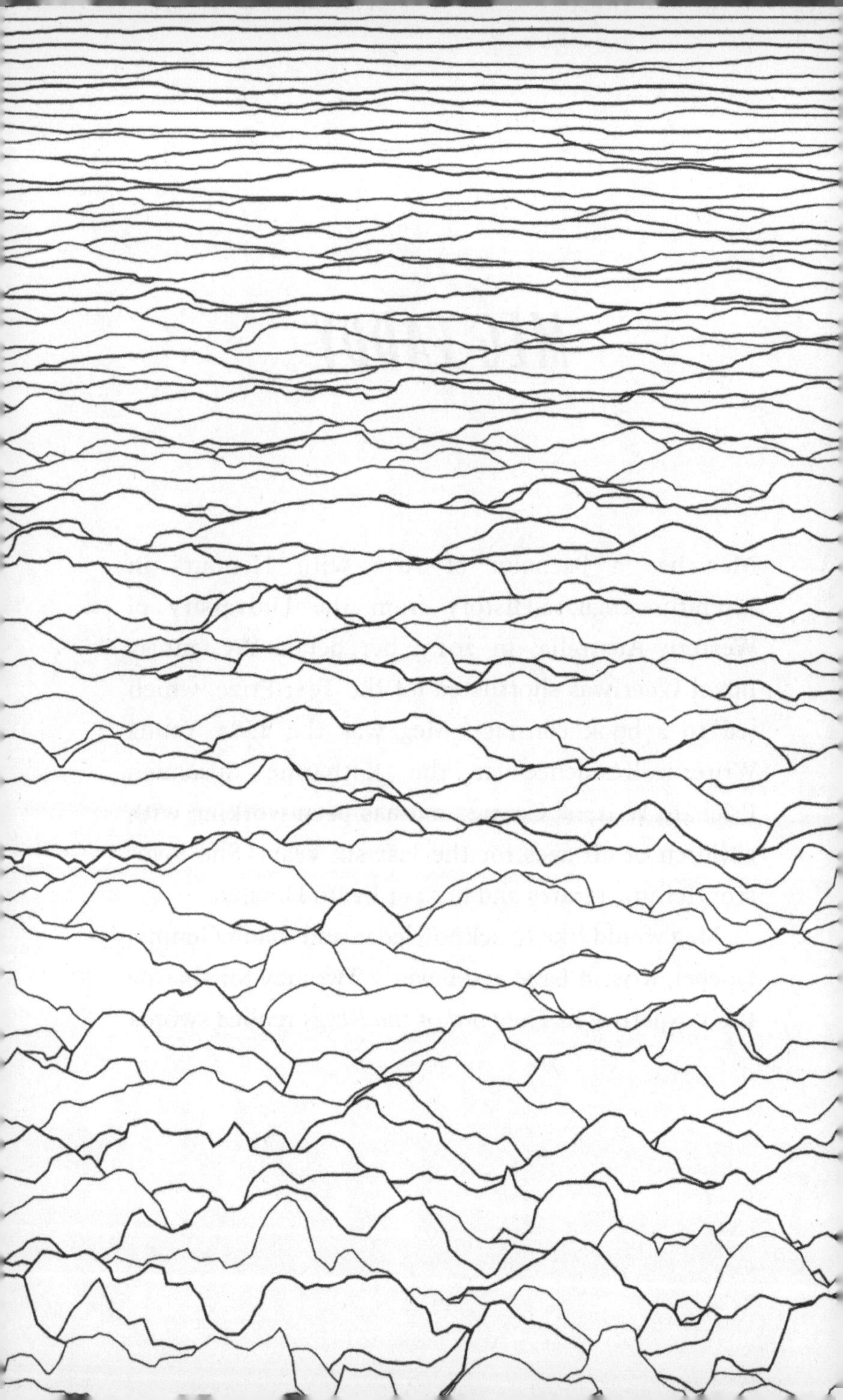

BLUE'S DOOR

Most of the shells around here are flat and empty. They're split angel-wings, pipis and the occasional mother-of-pearl abalone husk. My younger brother, tow-headed and chubby, delights in them. He hops behind me with open palms, scooping the bland discs into his hands along with clotted sand.

I search for a rarer prize. I want shells that hold the ocean, shells that sing the waves into your ear even if you happen to be standing in the hills far away. Every day after school, I walk our dog and my brother along the beach until we reach the spot where an old sailing ship is moored. I'm usually empty-handed at the end of the afternoon, but my brother has a growing collection of shells and sea-smoothed glass for our parents to coo over. They say this is the reason we moved to the coast, so Liam and I can enjoy a childhood roaming beaches and parks.

As Liam bends to claim a white cuttlefish, our dog stiffens. Her eyes are ahead. I follow her gaze and bend to toss her ears. Just another beachgoer.

The boy glances back as we near him, then turns properly to face us. He's tall and lanky, wearing skinny-leg jeans and a grey hoodie. He can't be much older than I am.

His face slips into a smile. 'Nice afternoon,' he says.

I nod and steer Liam away from him. Weirdo.

'Bit cold for a walk, though.'

I look over my shoulder and shrug. Stalker-weirdo.

'They call me Blue.'

I turn around, and the words *Get lost, Blue,* hover on my lips. Something in his gaze stops me. Easy to see why they call him Blue. His hair is tawny, but his eyes are pale. There's something different about him. Something I like.

'Hey, Blue.'

Liam is holding the sleeve of my hoodie now. He knows the rules about talking to strangers. The dog is just as concerned and she sniffs in Blue's direction but won't go near him.

Blue's smile fades.

'Sorry,' he says. 'I didn't mean to scare you.'

'Oh, no one's scared.' And I'm not. Self-defence classes are compulsory at my school.

'I just . . .' The sea crackles and hisses in the gaps between his words. 'I like your hoodie. *Lord of the Rings,* right?'

The white tree of Gondor is stamped onto my belly. I nod. His eyes brighten, and he pulls out a replica One Ring on a chain. What a geek. I warm to him.

'I'd like to know you.' He's so frank it catches me off-guard. Those words could be sleazy, unusual, but coming from him they're sweet. 'Will you be here tomorrow?'

'Could be.' I whistle for the dog, pull Liam's hand and walk on. I can feel Blue's eyes following me all the way along the beach.

We meet Blue again the next day, and I tell him my name the day after that. On the fourth day I leave Liam and the dog at home.

Winter is slumping into town, sullen and listless. By the time I meet Blue at the beach, my hair is salt-stiff and wisped back like fairy floss. It's not cold, but wind sends sand lashing across the beach, biting at my bare legs. Blue is animated, wild in the blustering weather. He's spindly like a daddy-long-legs. Most boys I know are creatures of weary disdain or stale vulgarity, but Blue's a hunter. At some moments he's still and quiet, padding across the beach with such intent, I half-expect to see a pointed fin rising from his back. Then, with spitfire quickness, he ducks and claims an abalone shell gleaming even in the dull light of the fading afternoon.

He matches my moods and movements. I'm not used to that.

'I collect things,' he tells me.

'What sort of things?'

'Everything. Shells, books, figurines . . .' His face opens into a grin as he looks at me sideways. 'Pretty girls.'

I flick water at him. His laugh hits me with a splash and it echoes somewhere just below my ribcage.

I want to see where he lives, absorb every facet of his existence until I am bloated and soft. I want assurance that he is like me, that we're meant for one another. But he's homeschooled, so it's hard to work my way into the centre of his life without visiting his house.

It takes weeks of whittling at him, kisses and bribes, but finally he leads me through the greying streets to his home. He walks a few paces ahead of me, his shirt pinned against his back by the wind coming off the sea. As the sky starts to spit, I want him to use his jacket to shield me from the rain.

But when he looks over his shoulder at me, I'm careful not to catch his eye.

I don't want to seem needy.

I know his front door before he points to it – a deep aged blue. And there's a jacaranda tree on the front verge. Blue unlocks the door and ushers me in, speaking in a hushed voice. For the first time, I realise he's nervous, agitated.

'Don't mind Mum,' he says. 'She gets a bit funny. We don't usually have visitors. Don't take it personally if she's unfriendly.'

It's dark inside, darker than I would have expected. Blue flicks a light switch, but the bulb goes out instantly, lightning-bright to dark again within a breath. Blue slaps the wall and walks ahead of me into the kitchen. I hear murmurs, and follow them. Hard to imagine Blue living here.

His mum sits in a wooden chair in the kitchen. Fat sags out of her; she looks like a water balloon with a string tied around the middle. Her body is an inert pool of flesh, barely contained by her clothing. She breathes through her mouth, loudly.

When she sees me she leans forwards. 'Sieben,' she slurs. Seven? My German is limited. I wonder if she speaks any English.

'Hello, Mrs Fitcher,' I say. It took me a week to get Blue's last name from him. 'How are you?'

'Sieben.' With monumental effort, she lifts an arm and points at me with sausage-like fingers. A laugh squeals from her nose and mingles with the sound of rain splattering against the windows.

I step back, awkward and frightened. I understand Blue's reluctance now. I wish he'd warned me better. My eyes stray towards the front door. Blue catches me looking.

'It's all right,' he says.

His mother lurches forwards and mumbles something, puffy lips pinching together and slackening as they form half-syllables. Blue leans in and listens. When he straightens and turns away from her, his face is twisted into an embarrassed grimace.

'I need to pick up Mum's prescription from the chemist. Come along?'

'You've got to be joking.' The rain whips against the roof and the panes. I'm not going out in that.

'I have an umbrella.' He grins. 'It'll be an adventure.'

No, it won't. It'll be cold and wet and the umbrella will turn inside out. And then we'll stop in some coffee shop until it's late, and I'll never get a chance to explore his house and see into his funny lock-box mind. I don't want to stay in the house alone with his mum, but the chemist is just down the road. It won't take him long.

'Have fun with that. I'm staying here. I want to explore your house.'

He laughs, but there is an odd ring to it. Maybe he's hurt that I'm not coming with him.

'You can explore all you want,' he says. 'Just . . . I hate to be a dork about this. Can you stay out of my collectibles room?' He nods towards an indigo door on our right.

I can't help but grin. 'You have a *collectibles* room?'

'Yeah. And I'd prefer it if you don't go in there.'

'Are you scared I'll break all your things?'

'I mean it.'

'Fine, you weirdo,' I say. 'Go on. I won't go into your "collectibles" room.'

A smile hovers over his lips. I almost run out the door after him, to take his hands and kiss him, but I manage to stand my ground.

Mrs Fitcher rocks forwards in her chair again, watching me with pale eyes. 'Sieben.'

'Sieben,' I repeat, distracted. I step towards the forbidden room and press my palm against the cool, smooth wood of the door. The only paint inside the house that isn't flaking or cracked. Blue's own little hobbit-hole. I won't touch anything, but I'm greedy for information. I just want to know who he is. Every detail.

I open the door and step in.

It's the Cave of Wonders, Smaug's hoard, a pirate's ransom. I forget Blue's hostility. It's washed away, swept from the bank at the sight of this trove.

All the *Harry Potter* wands are lined up along the wall. Replica swords from *Game of Thrones* and other fantasy epics. There are shelves of Lego models. 'Speak friend and enter' is written in Tengwar across a large cupboard, and there are stacks of books on Klingon and Elvish. The bin is in the shape of the TARDIS.

I grin. *Mega*-geek.

I make my way straight to the cupboard. It isn't locked, so he can't be too particular about whether people see inside. I pull open the doors, expecting to see more memorabilia. I feel the smile drop from my face.

He's been holding out on me all this time.

Hours and hours looking along the beach for the perfect shells, and here they are. Seven giant, gleaming-white turban shells. I've never seen such large shells before, except in the museum in the city.

My hands turn greedy. They curl about the first shell. The outside is rough and clean, and when I dip my finger inside it's smooth and creamy. I lift it to my ear, thirsting for the deep rasp of the ocean. I breathe in delight as the sound of waves fills me.

The sounds start to change. Gurgling. Hoarse

breaths. Erratic splashing, clearer than anything that should be coming from the inside of a shell.

Then screams.

I drop it. My hands are shaking. I grab the second and look it over. No batteries. No microphone. No recording. It's just a shell. But when I hold it to my ear, it's the same as the first. Shrieks. Waves. Gasping for air. Holding the second shell, I know I am hearing someone's last breath. Drowning? It sounds like drowning. I drop the shell and snatch up the third. The fourth. Fifth. Sixth.

The seventh shell is empty. Silent. Not even the usual gush of the ocean to break the stillness. All I can hear is my own breath, quick and frightened.

Seven.

'I told you I collect pretty girls.'

The shell clatters to the floor but does not break. I spin and face Blue. He closes the door behind him and smiles. His angel eyes are bright. On the other side of the door, I can hear his mother roaring the same number, over and over.

'What is this?' It's a miracle I can speak, and I don't know how my voice is so strong.

'I warned you. Just as I warned the other girls.' His teeth have never looked so sharp. 'No one can say I wasn't fair.'

The other girls. Seven shells, six other girls. There

are no windows in this room. How did I not notice before? Only one door.

Blue's lips are pinned back, his eyes too pale and too bright. He steps closer to me and stoops to claim the shell. Possibilities for escape run quickly through my mind: I'm smaller than he is and probably not as strong so there's no sense in tackling him. Before his hand gets to it, I kick the shell, send it sliding across the wooden floor. Blue lunges after it, and I lunge for the door. He's up in a second, though, grabbing my hood and dragging me to the floor. I hit the boards. Blue has the shell and he tries to grab my wrists, but the self-defence classes kick in. I flick my wrists around, freeing my hands and punch between his legs.

Whatever he is, whatever he can do, part of him must be human, because the punch works. He rolls away from me, groaning. I stagger to my feet, using the TARDIS bin as a prop. When Blue tries to follow, I throw the bin at him. Balls of paper and wrappers spill out. I race for the door, but he is there again, transformed, a hoarse laugh burbling from his lips. His gums are red. His skin is grey, and his hair looks like blood.

'As soon as I saw you, I knew you'd be fun,' he says. The smile drops away from his face. 'But the time for fun is over.' He bares his teeth and holds the shell out towards me. My skin jumps, wrenches, contorts.

It feels as though it will peel from my body. Hurts so much. I can't think, can't breathe. I choke and water bubbles out of my mouth.

I fling myself against the wall. My hand gropes blindly on the rack of weapons, and I pull away a sword. Heavy. With two hands, it's still hard to lift.

The shell tugs at me. It drags a wail from my lips.

'A sword?' Blue asks. His laugh is a rattle. 'Do you think you can run me through? It's a replica. The blade's hardly even sharp.'

I swing the sword. My muscles burn. I don't aim for Blue, but for the shell in his hand. The blade is so heavy that I can't aim properly. I hit his arm and he howls in anger. The shell clatters once more to the floor and I kick it under a chest of drawers. Blue charges at me. I step back, dragging the sword along the ground and move towards the cupboard. I've read enough books. I know how the stories go. I kick the cupboard door open. With one hand, I sweep the remaining shells off the shelves. I can hear them screaming. Six girls before me.

Blue grows, stretching and becoming thinner. He reeks of brine and fish. His skin is starting to come away from his bones. He is *rotting* in front of me.

'Put the sword down.' His tongue, serpentine, flicks around his lips.

'All right.' I slam the sword into the first shell.

It erupts, shatters, salty water bubbling out and creeping towards Blue as water leaks from his mouth. He brushes it away with an impatient hand.

I break the second shell. More water. Blue spits it out. The third. He's gagging now, and his eyes are wide. Panic. He reaches for me but I jump back, dragging the sword with me.

As I smash the fourth and fifth shells, Blue staggers and the water turns red as it gushes from his lips and nose. He is on his hands and knees now, choking on a scream. I hook my foot about the sixth shell and draw it closer to me, keeping my eyes on Blue a moment longer. His fingers have elongated into claws, and his mouth is filled with layers of teeth.

'No one's scared of you,' I rasp, and bring the sword down onto the sixth shell.

Blue howls. The sound is more than I can bear. I drop to my knees and clap my hands to my ears, closing my eyes. The world rocks and gushes around me.

When I open my eyes, Blue is gone. Only the salty, seething water remains.

Relief leaves me hollow. I inch away from the water as it pools over the floor. I don't want to touch it. I feel sick, and curling into a corner, I rest my forehead on my knees and breathe until the feeling returns to my arms.

I reach over and brush my fingers across the hilt of the sword that saved my life. Gandalf's 'Glamdring', from *The Lord of the Rings.* I curl my fingers about the hilt. It's mine now.

I crawl to the chest of drawers and fish around beneath it. My fingers close about the seventh shell – the shell Blue intended for me. I hold it tight as I struggle to my feet and limp out of the room.

Blue's mother stares at me, her laughter subdued. She splutters a moment, eyes goggling, then chokes out a question.

'Sieben?'

I turn and walk down the hall, leaving her in the darkness. My back aches. My hip is bruised, and my arms are heavy with pain. I can hardly hold the sword now, but I'm not about to let it go.

The wind and the rain batter me as I push through the door and onto the street. My heart squishes a double beat through my ears, dull and rapid. Spitting gruel-like water onto the pavement; a car slows as it goes by. A guy in a snap-back cap gapes out the window at me. The girl dragging a sword along the footpath.

I squint into the rain and limp towards the beach. The sword scrapes along a flagstone, clips as I step off the path, and makes a dry rasp along the wet sand. The salt air cracks my lips and smacks my cheeks.

Setting Blue's shell down on a rock, I heave Glamdring one last time and bring it down until his remnants are reduced to shards and dust. I gather the pieces and stumble past the lip of the waves to stand shin-deep, my jeans heavy as the water soaks through. My fingers tremble about the shell fragments until I wind back my arm and pitch them into the ash-grey sea. They bob on the surface a second, then sink. No more shells, no more Blue. He's gone, reclaimed by the ocean.

The drowning girls, though, they stay with me.

Every wave sounds like a scream.

Barry is the multi-award-winning author of eighteen novels for young adults and children. His books have been translated into eight languages and published in fourteen countries. Barry lives in Darwin in the Northern Territory with his wife, Nita, and a deranged blue heeler called Zorro.

THE PALE MAN

I have seen the pale man only four times in my life, but sometimes I think I've lived with him for most of my sixteen years.

The first time, I couldn't have been more than five or six and, looking back on it, I'm not even sure it *was* the pale man. For one thing I was sick, running a high fever, though this is something I've only pieced together later in conversations with Mum. What I *do* remember is lying in bed, cuddling a battered teddy bear, and staring into darkness, haunted by a fear common to small kids – the tingling dread that can so easily tip over into full-blown panic. Something was in my bedroom with me and that something – the stuff of countless childhood nightmares – was hiding in the wardrobe.

I was aware at first of a small movement, though possibly movement is too strong a word. Maybe it was more a sense of gathering within the darkness behind the slightly open door, a notion that eyes were fixed on me, that at any moment a horror might erupt from that hiding place. No, that it *would* burst out. A monster with red eyes and sharpened teeth and long talons, but it was waiting patiently until I closed my eyes. My only defence was keeping them open. As long as I stared at the door it would be forced to stay behind it. My life, at the very least my sanity, was dependent upon that concentration.

The door to my wardrobe swung open, so slowly it had to be a deliberate ratcheting up of my terror. Mum and Dad told me later the wardrobe would often swing open by itself, that there was something wrong with the hinges and the house we lived in was prone to random gusts and eddies of wind.

I don't believe it.

Something had opened my wardrobe door and, as my eyes fixated on the darkness within, I began to see it there beneath the hanging T-shirts and shorts and coats, crouched in a nest of shadows. Eyes. Not red but pale, so pale, and fixed on mine. The suggestion of a head and body attached to those eyes, something equally pale, like it had never been kissed by sunshine but leached of colour from an existence lived entirely beneath the earth, amongst the worms and crawling creatures that feed on dead flesh.

I knew I was defenceless, at the mercy of the pale evil, whose hand, as I watched and laboured for breath, curled around the edge of the wardrobe door as if to find purchase in my world.

'Danny, it's okay. Just a bad dream, that's all. Just a bad dream.' Mum held me close and I supposed I must have screamed. She opened the wardrobe and showed me, in a bright light that banished all shadows, how the wardrobe held nothing but coats and T-shirts and shorts. But I think I knew, even then, that what had waited for me hadn't gone away. Not really. It was still there, biding its time.

'My God,' said Mum. 'You're burning up.'

I was covered in sweat. It's what terror does.

The second time I saw the pale man, I was about twelve. On this occasion he was more than a vague presence. And he turned up during the day.

We had gone on holiday, rented a cottage somewhere in rural Victoria. Just the three of us, which, to be honest, was really boring. I was away from friends, my computer and everything that gave life meaning. And what did I get in return? Trees and long walks.

On the third day, Mum and Dad suggested another trek, even though we'd done one the day before. And the day before that. I argued.

'What's the point?' I said. 'It's not like we're gonna see anything different from what we saw yesterday. Trees, paths and birds. I saw them. I don't want to see them again.'

Dad argued back. The joys of walking, the wonder of nature, the fresh air in such short supply at our city home, spending quality time as a family. I wasn't buying it. In the end they took off by themselves and I settled down to watch the television – the only thing in the cottage that met with my approval.

At first it was just a flicker in my peripheral vision, a slight blur from the window that *could* have been someone walking past. Or maybe a bush or tree moving in the wind. But I didn't think there were any trees or bushes directly outside the building. And the cottage was isolated. I tried to ignore it, put it down to imagination, but the next time the blur came from the opposite window, as if someone or something was circling the house. I snapped my head around, but I was too late. A shape – not even that, not even as defined as a shape – seemed to have ghosted past the window frame. The house took on a chill and the air was heavy with . . . possibilities.

I opened the front door and looked outside. Twelve

years old, too old to be spooked by ghosts and demons, particularly in full sunshine. So I told myself at the time. But I felt something like an itch below my shoulder blades, as if eyes were trained on my back. I spun around. Nothing. I scanned the house and garden. Nothing moved and I couldn't hear any bird calls. It was like the world was holding its breath. Suddenly, taking a walk with my parents seemed the most attractive thing in the world.

There. Just turning the corner off to my right. A pale form, but then it disappeared. Did I see it or was my imagination forming images, manufacturing something from nothing? I ran then, to the corner where the thing had vanished. This was not courage, this was movement, and I craved it. But as I reached the corner, the idea that something would step out in front of me, that I would collide with a nightmare, made my skin crawl.

Again, nothing.

I stood for a moment, wondering what to do. Chasing a shadow around the walls of the building seemed absurd and, anyway, approaching another corner without knowing what was around it was more than I could bear. Go back inside? What if the intruder – I was thinking intruder, maybe a homeless man or maybe, just maybe, someone with a boning knife and dead eyes and a lust to spill blood – what if he had already slipped through the open door and was waiting for me?

I backed away from the cottage.

The garden was large and mainly given over to grass, but there was a tree perhaps fifty metres away. I stood in its shade and watched the house. From that distance and angle I would be able to see if someone approached me, but that didn't stop me from glancing behind occasionally. The longer I stood, the more I dreaded the feeling of a bony hand clamped on my shoulder.

A flash of movement from a window, a curtain that lifted and fell. My heart thudded and a roaring filled my ears. I watched.

I understand what you are thinking. A small boy, alone and prey to an overactive imagination. I understand, but I can only tell you what I saw.

A face appeared in my bedroom window. A head unnaturally long and hairless, a slit for a mouth and two holes for a nose. Deathly pale. A hand lifted the curtain to the side as if to afford a better view of the garden, of the tree, of me. The man's eyes – I knew it was a man, but I can't say why – were as pale as the flesh of his face and hand, so they were not really distinguishable as a feature at all. Bone-white and cold as the moon. I was pinned by its stare, like a dead insect.

I don't remember running. I don't remember whether it was easy to find my parents or whether I just stumbled upon them as they returned from their walk. I have little recollection of my hysteria. All I know is that I never went back into that house again, that I stayed locked and sobbing in the car while my parents packed everything up and took us home. Dad was grim-faced all the way back. Mum was simply worried. I had destroyed the family holiday.

No one asked me to take responsibility, though Dad's silence spoke volumes. As far as I was concerned, if it was anyone's fault, it was the pale man's.

Fifteen years old and another bright day. I was playing cricket for the local under-sixteen team and we were chasing 165 to win. I was on 42 not out, we were four wickets down and cruising. It was one of those days when you see the ball really well and it was hitting the middle of the bat so beautifully you couldn't tell you'd even hit it before the ball raced over the boundary rope.

The opposing team had brought on their fast bowler for a second spell. Long, gangly guy, tricky in terms of pace but straight up and down, no movement through the air or off the pitch. I could handle him. Before I took guard, I asked for the sightscreen to be moved a little, since he was going to be bowling round the wicket, then checked out the field placings.

The bowler was only a few metres from the popping crease when a movement close to the sightscreen made me back away from the stumps. The bowler wasn't happy. He was part way through his delivery stride and couldn't stop. He ended up, the ball still in his hand, almost in my face, his own red and flushed.

'Shit, man,' he said. 'What the hell you doin'? You can't just bale out like that.'

'Sorry,' I said. 'Movement behind your arm.'

He looked towards the sightscreen. There weren't many spectators about – just some mums and dads, the occasional friend of one of the players. It was deserted behind the bowler.

'Yeah, right,' he said. 'You watch too much television, mate. Think you're Dave Warner or something.'

'Look, I saw something move . . .' But I didn't get a chance to finish the sentence. The pale man moved out from behind the sightscreen, stood on the rope, stared at me.

I had almost forgotten about him in those intervening three years.

Almost.

Now those fears came rushing back – the hand on the wardrobe, the shape against the bedroom window of a holiday home, dead eyes boring into mine, looking for a weakness and waiting, waiting.

'You all right, mate?' said the bowler. 'Look like you've seen a ghost.'

'What do you see there?' I pointed. The bowler followed my finger, then looked back at me. His face had regained most of its normal colour.

'A sightscreen, mate. What else is there to see?' I knew his answer before he spoke.

The umpires got involved at that point. It was clear something was wrong with me. My legs were shaking and I couldn't focus on anything other than the pale man standing motionless on the boundary and looking *through* the players and officials gathered around me, pale eyes boring into mine. One umpire fluttered his fingers in front of my face, but I didn't react. I suspect I didn't look crash-hot either, that I was as pale as that motionless form on the boundary rope.

In the end, they forced my retirement. Told me I wasn't fit to carry on batting, that I should get to a doctor as soon as possible. I was led to the dressing room, thankfully the opposite side of the ground to the pale man, and I didn't do myself any favours there, either. I walked backwards, never taking my eyes from his.

He didn't stop watching me either.

The only good thing about lying in a hospital bed for three weeks is that it gives you time to think.

For the first week I was here, I thought about nothing except the pale man and how he'd brought me to this pass, this pain, this mess that is my right leg. I didn't sleep much in those seven days and not just because of the agony that pulsed and probed, a red-hot poker below my knee. I relived images, constantly watching how it all unfolded.

I'd been waiting for the school bus, chatting to a couple of mates. A normal day in every way. When the bus rocked up there was a long line, mainly kids from my school. The bus was always packed at this time of the day. Forty passengers, if you want to be exact. I took out my pass and shuffled along the line, past the driver. Forty-one, if you count him. Would have been forty-two with me.

I glanced up towards the back of the bus. My mates and I tended to sit as far back as we possibly could, though I knew there was no chance this morning of taking the prized back seats. In fact, we'd be lucky to get a seat at all. Through the packed throng of bodies and school bags, I saw him rising up from the back seat.

The pale man.

He wore a suit, a black suit that made the dead pallor of his face stand out in greater contrast. The hairless head, the gash of a mouth open slightly to reveal one yellow tooth, the pale lidless eyes fixed on me.

He moved down the aisle towards me, impossibly fast, brushing past kids who didn't react. How could they not see him? The small part of my mind still functioning knew the answer. Because he wasn't there. Not really. He was only in my head, a creature I had created, a monster finally coming to get me, to settle an old score after waiting so patiently and for so long.

I can't remember what happened next, but I can imagine. Me turning around, pushing desperately past kids in the queue, knowing the pale man was coming towards me, that time was running out, that my only chance was to get off that bus and run, run, run. Can you outrun something in your mind? Probably not, but that didn't stop me. Breaking through the last group at the back of the line, finding space, dropping my school bag and running, across the road, not daring to look behind, not seeing the car that struck me a glancing blow, sending me first into oblivion and then a world of pain.

Two weeks of different thinking.

I talked to Mum. She wasn't sure about the timing, but I think I know. That night when I was six, the monster in the cupboard, the fever that apparently nearly killed me. Might have killed me if my parents hadn't got me to the hospital in time. And they only woke up and realised how sick I was because I screamed in the middle of the night. The cricket game? Here's how it *might* have played out. The bowler running in, a short-pitched ball rearing up from the pitch, me ducking but too late. Players running in as I lay on the popping-crease, an ambulance, lights flashing, sirens blaring, but that was too late as well. The cottage? Ah, this is where I have to guess. Maybe a gas leak waiting for an electrical switch to be turned on, a spark that ushered an orange and red oblivion. Or perhaps a genuine intruder, one of flesh and blood, coming that day or the next with an axe or a shotgun or a thin, sharp blade. I will never know. But I am convinced *something* would have happened.

I know what angels are supposed to look like, but I've seen mine and he is pale and terrible.

The brakes failed on that school bus, the one that took off without me. It smashed into a pillar on the freeway, burst into flames and snuffed out forty-one lives. The news said they died instantly.

And me? I lie in my hospital bed and think about the pale man.

ALI COBBY ECKERMANN

Ali, poet and writer, was born on Kaurna country, and grew up on Ngadjuri country, South Australia. She has travelled extensively and lived most of her adult life on Arrernte country, Jawoyn country and Larrakia country in the Northern Territory. Eckermann met her birth mother, Audrey, when she was in her 30s and learnt that her mob was Yankunytjatjara from north-west South Australia.

YANKUNYTJATJARA LOVE POEMS

ngayulu tjina ananyi south
  ngayulu tjina ananyi north
where are you my Warrior?

ngayulu nyinakatinyi desert
  ngayulu nyinakatinyi ocean
where are you my Warrior?

ngayulu inma ankanyi trees
  ngayulu inma ankanyi rocks
where are you my Warrior?

YANKUNYTJATJARA LOVE POEMS

I walk to the south
  I walk to the north
where are you my Warrior?

I sit with the desert
  I sit with the ocean
where are you my Warrior?

I sing to the trees
  I sing to the rocks
where are you my Warrior?

ngayulu inmaku pakani birds
  ngayulu inmaku pakani animals
where are you my Warrior?

ngura ilkaritja everywhere
where are You?

I will show you a field of zebra finch Dreaming
  in the shadow of the *puli puli* ochre
when the soft blanket of language hums kinship
  and campfires flavour windswept hair

little girls stack single twigs on embers under
  tjamus skin of painted love
the dance of *kalaya* feathers will sweep
  the *munda* with your smile

do not look at me in daylight; that
  gift comes in the night
tomorrow I will show *ngunytju* our
  marriage proposal in my smile

in the cave she rolls *puli pulka* for table, for
  tjulpun tjulpun they pick for each another
she carries *piti tjuta* filled with river
  sand to soften the hard rock floor

I dance with the birds
  I dance with the animals
where are you my Warrior?

Heaven is everywhere
where are You?

I will show you a field of zebra finch Dreaming
  in the shadow of the stony hill ochre
when the soft blanket of language hums kinship
  and campfires flavour windswept hair

little girls stack single twigs on embers under
  Grandfather's skin of painted love
the dance of emu feathers will sweep
  the red earth with your smile

do not look at me in daylight; that
  gift comes in the night
tomorrow I will show Mother our
  marriage proposal in my smile

in the cave she rolls the big rock for table, for
  the desert wildflowers they pick each another
she carries many coolamons filled with river
  sand to soften the hard rock floor

she makes shelf from braided *punu* to hold
  nyalpi tjuta given by the message birds
when he sleeps she polishes his weapons with
  goanna and emu fat till they glisten in fire light

he tells the story of the notches on his spear,
  the story of the maps on his woomera
their *kuru* fill with spot fires lit on his return

the other *kungkas* laugh 'get over yourself'
  they laugh 'he's not that good'
she smiles she knows him in the night

there is love in the wind by the singing rock
down the river by the ancient tree
love in *malu ngintaka* and *kalaya*
love when spirits speak no human voice
at the sacred sites eyes unblemished
watch *walawaru* soar over hidden *kapi*
find the *mukuringanyi*

she makes shelf from braided saplings to hold
   all the feathers given by the message birds
when he sleeps she polishes his weapons with
   goanna and emu fat till they glisten in fire light

he tells the story of the notches on his spear,
   the story of the maps on his woomera
their eyes fill with spot fires lit on his return

the other women laugh 'get over yourself'
   they laugh 'he's not that good'
she smiles she knows him in the night

there is love in the wind by the singing rock
down the river by the ancient tree
love in kangaroo goanna and emu
love when spirits speak no human voice
at the sacred sites eyes unblemished
watch wedge tail eagle soar over hidden water
find the love

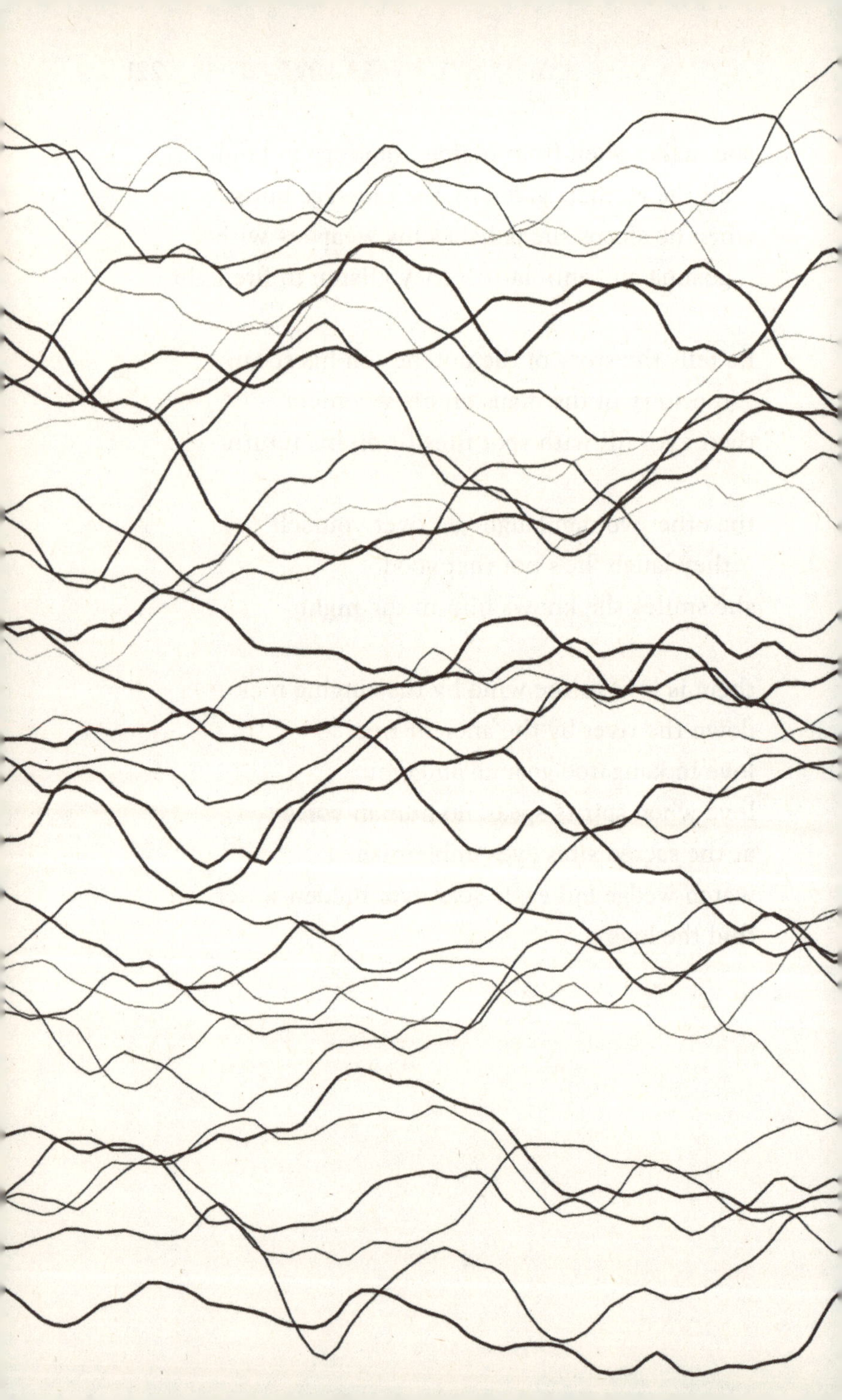

TONY BIRCH

Tony was born in inner-city Melbourne, into a large family of Aboriginal, West Indian and Irish descent. Much of Tony's challenging childhood is captured in the semi-autobiographical book *Shadowboxing*, where this short story was first published.

Tony writes short fiction, novels and essays and is also an educator and teacher of writing and history. He is passionate about social justice, creativity, mutual respect and recognition, the three Rs – reading, riting and running.

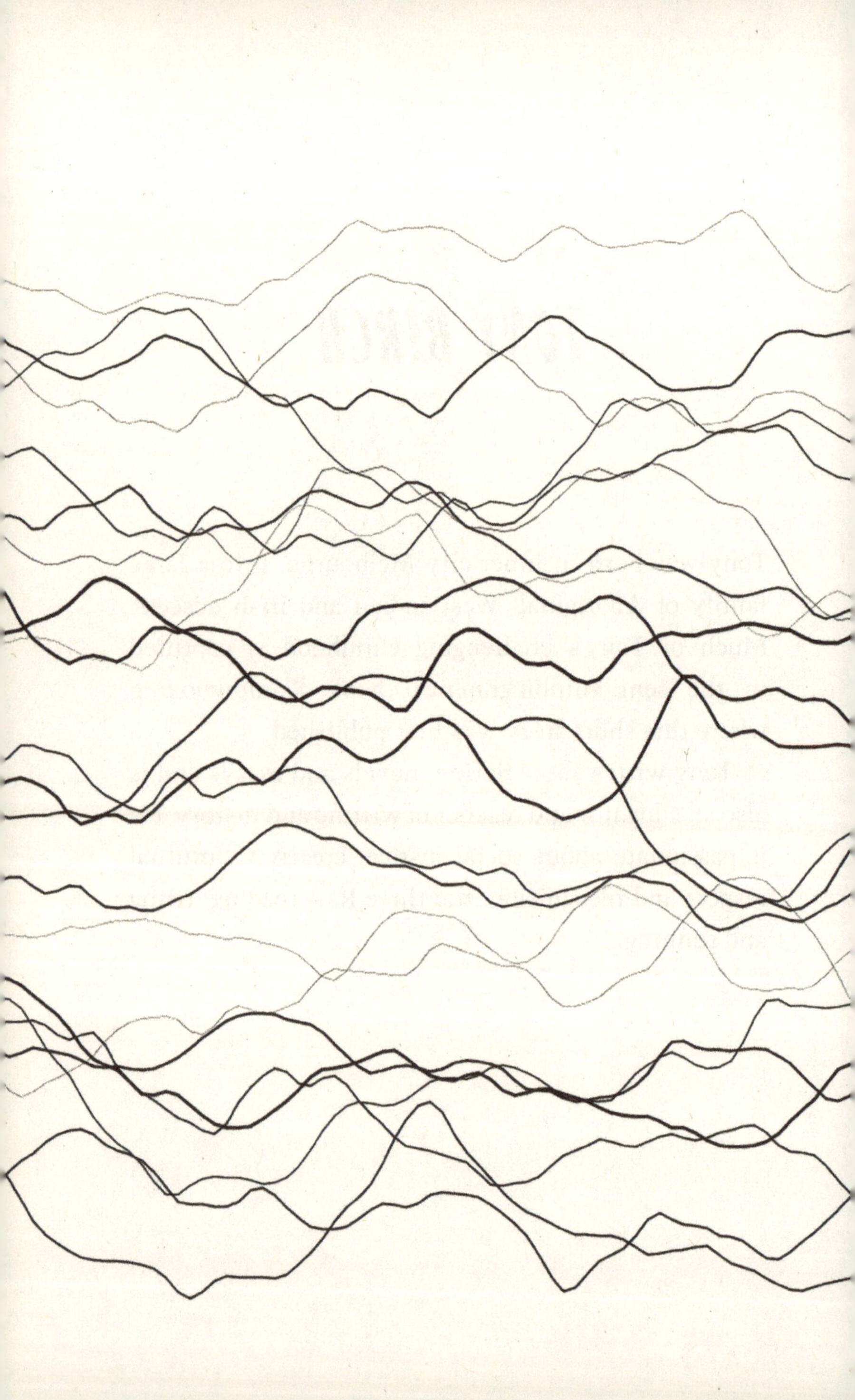

THE BUTCHER'S WIFE

I was on my way home on the last day of the school year when I saw her. I was coming out of the corner shop just as she was going in, carrying her baby under her arm. I caught only a glimpse of her face as we passed each other, but I noticed it immediately. I didn't really want to look, yet I found it just as hard to look away from her.

Her bruises were probably less than a week old and any swelling that she may have suffered had gone. And there were no obvious cuts. She had done a reasonably good job disguising the mottled blue-yellow patches around her eyes with a heavy foundation of powder. It was probably the same one my mum used.

But the layers of make-up never quite did the job.

The shadows under the surface always managed to give themselves away. I had seen the same shadows around my mother's eyes as she waited for me after school, on the opposite side of the road from the gate.

I took a final look at the butcher's wife. She looked back at me. I am still not sure why, but I smiled at her. She lowered her eyes, at her crying baby, while rocking her awkwardly up and down. It was then that I noticed that there was some swelling and a small cut above one eye – a small curved cut. That would have happened when she was hit by the edge of his wedding ring. I had also seen that before.

Her battered face would have surprised no one in the street. It was common to hear her screams coming from their house, accompanied by the swearing and abuse of her husband. In the following days the results of his handiwork would be displayed all over her face for the entire street to see.

He wasn't the only one who did that, of course. My father was the same. Most men around here, they were the same, most commonly after they had been drinking. But not my dad. He did not need the drink in him. And he gave no reasons either.

More and more, he enjoyed using mum as an occasional punching bag. He had done that the last time when she was pregnant, and all because she was a half-hour late home from the shops to prepare his tea.

I cannot remember seeing him hit her, that night, but I have not forgotten running into the kitchen, with Katie skipping behind me, and seeing her pinned to the floor beneath him. He had a knee wedged between her legs. Mum screamed at me to get Katie out of the room. I took her by the hand and we ran out and went to sit on the front doorstep together. All I could think about was that there was a baby just there, on the other side of my mother's stomach, where he had forced his knee. I knew that because when my mother was pregnant with Katie I would lie on the bed with her and she would lift her dress and let me feel Katie kicking on the other side. And Katie had done the same with this baby.

But this baby did not come. After that night my mother got sick. There were no more kicks to feel. The baby was gone.

My father was not like the butcher. He did not need the drink in order to strike out. But it helped. Saturday night was his night of the week. It was when hc was at his most unpredictable and destructive. On Sunday mornings we would assess the damage that he had left for us. He would sleep in, while Katie and I were sent off to mass, and mum cleaned the mess away.

Behind closed doors along the street many women went through the same ritual as my mother: mending a broken vase and making up a blackened eye. And no one said a word about it. Years later my mother told me that after he started hitting her she asked an older woman at work what she could do to stop him. She was told to stay out of his way as best she could. And other than that: 'Get used to it, love. It passes as they get older. They get slower and soften with the years. Or if you're real lucky, they drop dead.'

The butcher was not close to softening. He was a hard man, with muscled arms to rival my father's. He left early of a morning for work at the abattoir and did not get home of a night until after the pub had closed, just after six o'clock, ready to have a go at anyone.

In summer I slept on the sleep-out on our verandah. I would often wake during the night to the cries of the butcher's wife. I was never sure at first if the noise was coming from across the street or from my own house. It was not until I shook myself awake and trained my ear that I could go back to sleep, reassured that on this night, it was not my mother who was being beaten.

It was a warm night, between Christmas and New Year. The coming school year still seemed like a century away, and the factories had turned off their machines and closed their doors for the break. It was time to relax. Except for my father, whose work on the road crew was at its busiest during the holiday season. He stayed inside the house alone, drinking in the kitchen.

Almost everyone else had moved their lives into the street for the night in an effort to escape the heat of the narrow terraces. A radiogram up on the next corner was spinning rock'n'roll records. Lots of kids were out in the street playing under water hoses, while empty beer bottles were quickly mounting in a stack in the gutter.

I was standing behind Katie, wearing only my bathers, running a gentle stream of water over her head with the hose as she sat splashing around in our tin laundry tub. I had one eye on Katie and the other on my mother. She had dragged a kitchen chair into the street and was straddled across it while brushing her hair. She was wearing her favourite floral-print dress. She looked beautiful.

A breeze drifted down the middle of the street. It was lazy and sweet and warm. The sun was about to go down, but it did not look as if anybody was ready to give up on the street for the night. Katie jumped out of the trough and watched mum as she tossed her long, dark hair from side to side, catching the afterglow of the setting sun.

It was then that we heard the screams. Instinctively I turned around and looked across the road towards the open door of the butcher's house. Most everybody on the street did the same. I then heard a second scream followed by an inaudible bark from the butcher, and then the familiar thud of her body bouncing off a wall.

She ran from the house and into the street. Her face was covered in blood. She lost her footing and fell over, into the gutter. She managed to get to her hands and knees just as the butcher emerged from the house. He was carrying a trouser belt in one hand. We could hear the baby crying from somewhere inside the house.

The butcher's wife looked up at him, but did not try to get to her feet. She did not move at all. She remained perfectly still, as if she were attempting to make herself invisible. The butcher walked out onto the footpath towards his wife and stood over her with hands on his hips. He then looked across the street to those of us watching.

Even before he started hitting her with the belt, most people along the street were already collecting their kids under one arm and their chair in the other before disappearing inside and slamming their front doors behind them. Somebody had turned the radiogram off. I could hear it being dragged back into the house.

Each time that she tried to get to her feet the butcher whipped her with the trouser belt. I looked away and stared deeply into the floral pattern of my mother's dress. Katie began to cry. My mother looked at her and then up and down the street before getting to her feet.

She had taken only one step forward, in the direction of the butcher, when we heard his voice.

'Come on inside.' It was my father standing behind us.

My mother did not move, so he repeated himself. 'Come on in. It's late. Get the kids in.'

She looked at him pleadingly. She wanted him to do something, to intervene.

'Mick, please.'

He knew what she wanted. He looked across the road to the butcher. My father looked down at Katie, and then at my mother again.

'It's over, anyway. Come on in.'

The butcher looked proud of himself as he stood in the street with the belt hanging from his hand. He puffed his chest out. His wife got to her hands and knees, and peered up and down the street through a veil of hair hanging over her eyes. She slowly got to her feet. Blood was running from both her nose and mouth. Her dress, also covered in blood, was ripped from one shoulder to below her waist. She was wearing a white bra. It was also smudged with blood.

She wiped blood from her face with her forearm. She looked down at the blood smeared across her skin.

She then spat more blood from her mouth into the gutter. It ran away with the water from some kid's play-hose. The butcher's wife then scanned the street, looking into the eyes of those who had just witnessed what had occurred.

The butcher grabbed her by the arm and pushed her towards the house. She swung her arm at him and refused to move. It was only then that he looked uncomfortable and slightly embarrassed. He pushed her slightly in the back.

'Get going.'

She began to walk towards the house but then stopped again and looked over her shoulder at the street. We collectively looked the other way. She wiped her hand across her face one more time, and walked back into the house.

I lay on my bunk in the sleep-out later that night, unable to sleep. Family arguments could be heard up and down the street. I finally got to sleep, but woke during the night to the sound of a stray cat's purring. It had settled on the end of my bed. I was about to give it a good kick with the ball of my foot when I heard somebody walking by the house. I sat up in bed. The footsteps were followed by a second sound that I could not identify. I looked out through the louvre window. Someone was walking along the other side of the road towards Gertrude Street. It was the butcher's wife. And she was pushing her pram. It looked as if she had finally decided to escape from her husband.

I looked down to the end of the bed at the cat. It looked back at me through its one open eye. I let it stay there and fell back to sleep.

ANDREA HIRATA

Andrea was born in East Sumatra, Indonesia. He received a scholarship to study at Sheffield Hallam University, UK, majoring in economic theory.

In 2004, while volunteering for tsunami disaster relief in Aceh, he saw many ruined schools. He was reminded of an old promise he had made to his Fifth Grade teacher, Muslimah, where he vowed to one day write a book for his educator. Andrea started writing his first novel called *Laskar Pelangi: The Rainbow Troops*, which has been adapted for a feature film, television series and musical theatre.

TEN NEW STUDENTS

That morning, when I was just a boy, I sat on a long bench outside a school. The branch of an old filicium tree shaded me. My father sat beside me, hugging my shoulders as he nodded and smiled to each parent and child sitting on the bench in front of us. It was an important day: the first day of elementary school.

At the end of those long benches was an open door, and inside was an empty classroom. The doorframe was crooked. The entire school, in fact, leaned as if it would collapse at any moment. In the doorway stood two teachers, like hosts welcoming guests to a party. There was an old man with a patient face, Bapak K. A. Harfan Effendy Noor, or Pak Harfan – the school principal – and a young woman wearing a *jilbab*, or headscarf, Ibu N. A. Muslimah Hafsari, or Bu Mus for short. Like my father, they were smiling.

Yet Bu Mus's smile was a forced smile: she was apprehensive. Her face was tense and twitching nervously. She kept counting the number of children sitting on the long benches, so worried that she didn't even care about the sweat pouring down onto her eyelids. The sweat smudged her powder makeup, streaking her face and making her look like the queen's servant in *Dul Muluk*, an ancient play in our village.

'Nine people, just nine, Pamanda Guru, still short one,' she said anxiously to the principal. Pak Harfan stared at her with an empty look in his eyes.

I, too, felt anxious. Anxious because of the restless Bu Mus, and because of the sensation of my father's burden spreading over my entire body. Although he seemed at ease this morning, his rough arm hanging around my neck gave away his quick heartbeat. It wasn't easy for a forty-seven-year-old miner with a lot of children and a small salary to send his son to school. It would have been much easier to send me to work as a helper for a Chinese grocery stall at the market, or to the coast to work as a coolie to help ease the family's financial burdens. Sending a child to school meant tying oneself to years of costs, and for our family that was no easy matter.

My poor father.

I didn't have the heart to look him in the eye.

My father wasn't the only one trembling. The faces of the other parents showed that their thoughts, like my father's, were drifting off to the morning market as they imagined their sons better off as workers. These parents weren't convinced that their children's education, which they could afford only up to junior high, would brighten their families' futures. This morning they were forced to be at this school, either to avoid reproach from government officials for not sending their children to school, or to submit to modern demands to free their children from illiteracy.

I knew all of the parents and children sitting in front of me – except for one small dirty boy with curly red hair, trying to wriggle free from his father's grasp. His father wasn't wearing shoes and had on cheap cotton pants.

The rest of them were my good friends. Like Trapani sitting on his mother's lap, or Kucai sitting next to his father, or Sahara, who earlier had gotten very angry at her mother because she wanted to go into the classroom quickly, or Syahdan, who wasn't accompanied by anyone. We were neighbors, Belitong-Malays from the poorest community on the island. As for this school, Muhammadiyah Elementary, it, too, was the poorest, the poorest village school in

Belitong. There were only three reasons why parents enrolled their children here. First, Muhammadiyah Elementary didn't require any fees, and parents could contribute whatever they could afford whenever they could do so. Second, parents feared that their children had weak character and could easily be led astray by the devil, so they wanted them to have strong Islamic guidance from a young age. Third, their children weren't accepted at any other school.

Bu Mus, who was growing increasingly fretful, stared at the main road, hoping there would still be another student. Seeing her empty hope scared us. The South Sumatra Department of Education and Culture had issued a warning: If Muhammadiyah Elementary School had fewer than ten new students, then it, the oldest school in Belitong, would be shut down. Therefore Bu Mus and Pak Harfan were worried about expenses, and we – the nine small children caught in the middle – were worried we may not get to go to school at all.

Last year Muhammadiyah Elementary had only eleven students. Pak Harfan was pessimistic this year. He had secretly prepared a school-closing speech.

'We will wait until eleven o'clock,' Pak Harfan said to Bu Mus and the already hopeless parents. We were silent. Bu Mus's face was puffy from holding back tears. Today was her first day as a teacher, a moment she had been dreaming of for a very long time. She had just graduated from Sekolah Kepandaian Putri (Vocational Girls' School), a junior high school in the capital of the regency, Tanjong Pandan. She was only fifteen. She stood like a statue under the bell, staring out at the wide schoolyard and the main road. No one appeared. The sun rose higher to meet the middle of the day. Waiting for one more student was like trying to catch the wind.

The other children and I felt heartbroken. Our heads hung low.

At five till eleven, Bu Mus could no longer hide her dejection. Her big dreams for this poor school were about to fall apart before they could even take off, and thirty-two faithful years of Pak Harfan's unrewarded service were about to come to a close.

'Just nine people, Pamanda Guru,' Bu Mus said. She wasn't thinking clearly, repeating the same thing everyone already knew.

Finally, time was up. It was already five after eleven and the total number of students still did not equal ten. I took my father's arm off of my shoulders. Sahara sobbed in her mother's embrace. She wore socks and shoes, a *jilbab*, a blouse, and she also had books, a water bottle, and a backpack – all were new.

Pak Harfan went up to the parents and greeted them one by one. It was devastating. The parents patted him on the back to console him, and Bu Mus's eyes glistened as they filled with tears. Pal Harfan prepared to give his final speech. When he went to utter his first words, '*Assalamu alaikum.* Peace be upon you,' Trapani yelled and pointed to the edge of the schoolyard, startling everyone.

'Harun!'

We turned to look. Off in the distance was a tall, skinny boy, clumsily headed our way. His clothes and hairstyle were very neat. He wore a long-sleeved white shirt tucked into his shorts. His knees knocked together when he moved, forming an X as his body wobbled along. A plump middle-aged woman was trying with great difficulty to hold on to him. That boy was Harun, a funny boy and a good friend of ours. He was already fifteen years old, the same age as Bu Mus, but a bit behind mentally. He was extremely happy and half running, as if he couldn't wait to get to us. His mother stumbled after him, trying to hold on to his hand.

They were both nearly out of breath when they arrived in front of Pak Harfan.

'Bapak Guru,' said his mother, gasping for breath. 'Please accept Harun. The special-needs school is all the way on Bangka Island. We don't have the money to send him there. And more importantly, it's better that he's here at this school rather than at home, where he just chases my chicks around.'

Harun smiled widely, showing his long yellow teeth.

Pak Harfan was smiling, too. He looked over to Bu Mus and shrugged. 'It makes ten,' he said.

Harun had saved us! We clapped and cheered. Sahara, who couldn't sit any longer, stood up straight to fix the folds on her *jilbab* and firmly threw on her backpack. Bu Mus blushed. Her tears subsided, and she wiped the sweat from her powder-smudged face.

ABOUT THE EDITORS

Dr Susan La Marca is a consultant in the areas of children's and young adult literature and school libraries. She is currently Head of Library and Information Services at Genazzano FCJ College in Melbourne, and also an adjunct lecturer in the School of Information Studies at Charles Sturt University.

Susan is the editor of *Synergy*, the research journal of the School Library Association of Victoria and the Regional Director for Oceania of the International Association of School Librarianship. She is also the co-author of *Knowing Readers: Unlocking the Pleasures of Reading* and the author of *Designing the Learning Environment.*

Dr Pam Macintyre teaches language and literacy and children's and young adult literature at RMIT University. She has been a judge for the Victorian

Premier's Literary Awards, Aurealis Awards and the Children's Book Council of Australia Book of the Year Awards, and is the co-author of *Knowing Readers: Unlocking the Pleasures of Reading.*

Pam has been a recipient of the Dromkeen Librarian Award for Services to Children's Literature and the Leila St John Award for Distinguished Services to Children's Literature.

THINGS A MAP WON'T SHOW YOU

EDITED BY SUSAN LA MARCA AND PAM MACINTYRE

AN UNFORGETTABLE COLLECTION OF SHORT FICTION, POETRY AND COMIC ART FROM AUSTRALIA AND BEYOND . . .

A BOY WHO TRIES TO FLY, a cricket game in a refugee centre, a government guide to kissing, the perils of hunting goannas, an arranged marriage, an awkward blind date, a girl who stands on her head, an imprisoned king and a cursed Maori stone . . .

Sometimes funny, sometimes dramatic, always compelling, this collection featuring both established writers and emerging talent will broaden your horizons and excite your imagination.

INCLUDING: JAMES ROY * TANVEER AHMED * MICHAEL PRYOR * URSULA DUBOSARSKY * SONYA HARTNETT * DOUG MACLEOD * OLIVER PHOMMAVANH * BRENTON MCKENNA * TARA JUNE WINCH * SUDHA MURTY * OODGEROO NOONUCCAL